THE PENGUIN CLASSICS

FOUNDER EDITOR (1944–64): E. V. RIEU

PRESENT EDITORS
Betty Radice and Robert Baldick

PAULINE MATARASSO read modern languages
at Lady Margaret Hall, Oxford, and gained First
Class Honours in 1950. She was awarded a Doc-
torat de l'Université de Paris in 1958. Her thesis,
*Recherches historiques et littéraires sur 'Raoul de
Cambrai'*, was published in 1962. She has also
translated *The Quest of the Holy Grail* for the
Penguin Classics.

Aucassin and Nicolette

AND OTHER TALES

Translated by Pauline Matarasso

PENGUIN BOOKS

Penguin Books Ltd, Harmondsworth, Middlesex, England
Penguin Books Inc., 7110 Ambassador Road, Baltimore, Maryland 21207, U.S.A.
Penguin Books Australia Ltd, Ringwood, Victoria, Australia

—

Published in Penguin Books 1971
Copyright © Pauline Matarasso, 1971

—

Made and printed in Great Britain by
Richard Clay (The Chaucer Press) Ltd,
Bungay, Suffolk
Set in Monotype Fournier

TO MY FATHER
WITH LOVE

Contents

Preface

THIS collection of tales contains some of the best-known works
that the thirteenth century has bequeathed to us and others that,
after enjoying considerable popularity in their own day, have since
remained the preserve of scholars and connoisseurs. They have
been chosen for their intrinsic merit and because, within their
limited scope, they give a good picture of the society for whose
entertainment they were first composed.

The thirteenth century is one of those periodic high points where
history seems to pause for a moment before surrendering again to
the forces of change already latent in its deceptive equilibrium.
There is about its institutions, its thought and its art a feeling of
maturity. It was the age of the *Summa*, and what St Thomas was
doing for theology had its secular counterparts in that great com-
pendium of social mores, the Prose *Lancelot*, and that no less
remarkable lay encyclopedia, the *Roman de la Rose*. In literature,
it was an age of fulfilment rather than of innovation. And on a more
mundane plane it was the age that saw the emergence of a new read-
ing public. Alongside the aristocratic patrons (whose numbers were
continually increasing as the benefits of stability and economic ex-
pansion spread out in ever-widening ripples) there appeared a
rising middle class composed of functionaries and merchants. A
growing literacy in the higher reaches of society required to be fed,
and looked for a more varied fare than that provided by the *chansons
de geste*. It found its nourishment partly in the continuing, not to
say snowballing, output of Arthurian romances, partly in tales of
varied origin, some with highly exotic settings and improbable
plots, and others distinguished by a new realism, an acute observa-
tion of the social niceties and an assured technique that, at its best,
attains an almost classical elegance and sobriety. Most of these stor-
ies were written in the octosyllabic rhyming couplets adopted by
the earliest purveyors of courtly literature nearly a century before.
Their authors drew their subjects from many sources: popular

9

tales, antiquity, the rich store ferried from the East by pilgrims and Crusaders; they then applied their art and native gifts to refurbishing them and decking them out anew to suit contemporary taste. Although they were written to appeal to a medieval audience, their artistic merits ensure that many of them retain their freshness and their interest. Their appeal is not to the antiquarian alone. In that they deal with human problems they are timeless, and yet have the added charm of a window opened onto another world than ours.

The five tales in this collection were written within some fifty years of one another. In order to give the book some sort of unity I have made my selection from works which represent the more courtly trend in medieval literature, and among these the shorter. There are a great many romances whose prolixities and flights of fancy prevent their being of interest to any but students of the period. There is also a vast repertoire of short stories, or *fabliaux*, mostly constructed around a moral of the 'biter bit' variety, whose remarkable crudity is not always redeemed by an equal wit. The works presented here may thus be seen in the light of exceptions that confirm the rule. They stand apart from the romances by their relative brevity and the merits of their composition, and from most of the shorter tales by their tone and their literary aspirations. Indeed the best known, *Aucassin and Nicolette*, does not fall into any category; it is *sui generis* and must be considered apart. *The Chatelaine of Vergy* and *The Lay of the Reflection* were written for a courtly and essentially sophisticated public. Both are highly polished and skilfully constructed. They are the forerunners of the *conte*, the psychological short story. *The Dapple-grey Palfrey* and *The Count of Pontieu's Daughter* are more popular in tone and provide a certain welcome variety. The former is usually classed as a *fabliau*, but both its matter and its manner make it eminently suitable for inclusion here.

When one compares these stories with the Arthurian romances of Chrétien de Troyes and his successors, one is at once struck by their restraint and realism. There is no faery element here and no exoticism. Leaving aside for a moment the Never-Never-Land of *Aucassin and Nicolette*, the happenings are all on a human scale.

Preface

No giants stalk these pages, no damsels in distress lead wandering knights on perilous adventures. The overall effect puts one in mind of those miniatures of a slightly later date which decorate Books of Hours, where figures and background are intimately related, each explaining and determined by the other. In these stories the characters are the figures, the landscape is their social context; their freedom of action is hedged about by the proscriptions and *fiats* of the courtly code and all the limitations and obligations that a highly stratified society imposes on its members. But passions, when circumscribed, run just as deep, and those who violate the accepted rules are made to pay the ultimate price. This is the stern moral of *The Chatelaine of Vergy*, and one that the poet is at pains to emphasize. In *The Lay of the Reflection* the hero not only abides by the unwritten laws of courtly behaviour, he manipulates them to his own advantage with such consummate ease and elegance that they become, not a net in which to catch his feet and bring about his downfall, but a springboard to catapult him to success. In *The Dapple-grey Palfrey* the atmosphere is less rarified. The lovers here are less concerned with the refinements of the courtly ethic than with the more brutal logic of feudal power and the age-old opposition of rich fathers to penniless suitors, whatever their personal charms. It is worth noting, though, that the hero, a young man of impeccable ancestry, ends up not only with the damsel but with a large domain as well. The Middle Ages had little time for the Cinderella myth and even less for its obverse, the Princess and the Swineherd. Their concept of love was resolutely aristocratic. Even Nicolette turned out to be the daughter of the King of Carthage. Aucassin might declare himself indifferent to her parentage, but he was generally agreed to be a little odd, and the author had his public to consider; let alone his own views on the subject, perhaps reflected in his frequent references to her 'air of breeding'.

These five tales refract the past for us, each through its own particular prism. In *Aucassin and Nicolette* we are seeing society at a double remove, since it is more in the nature of a literary pastiche, itself poking fun at the extravagance latent in the courtly code and too often overtly displayed in the romances. *The Lay of the Reflection* and *The Chatelaine of Vergy* are among the most elegant literary expressions of that code. This is medieval society at its most sophisticated; but not perhaps, as regards the former, at its most idealized. There are those scholars who deny to the work of Jean Renart, the author of *The Lay of the Reflection*, the epithet of courtly. And indeed if one compares the attitudes of his knight and lady with those of, say, Lancelot and Guinevere as conceived by Chrétien, the difference is palpable enough. Gone are the total subjection of the lover, the deification of the lady; in their place we have a graceful fencing match, the attacker adroitly foiled and parried at every turn until by a master-stroke he wins the day. The underlying sensuality is scarcely veiled by the mannered tone, and the poet surveys the scene with amused detachment. None the less, if *The Dapple-grey Palfrey* can appropriately be called courtly (and it has been so designated) there is no reason to refuse the term to Renart's lay. With the exception of the author of *The Count of Pontieu's Daughter*, all these writers repeatedly use the epithet *courtois* to describe either themselves, their works or their heroes and heroines. It is therefore reasonable to infer that they saw themselves as treating certain subjects in a given style for a particular public. Their theme was love, and they were treating it in a courtly fashion for a public that would appreciate a refined and relatively idealized view of it. This is not to say that they were writing of courtly love in the tradition of the Provençal troubadours or as typified in certain works of Chrétien. The poet of *The Chatelaine of Vergy* was. So was Jean Renart, within the limits of his temperament, which did not predispose him to such views. But to set such narrow bounds to the concept of *courtoisie*, of which love, however integral an element, was not the whole, would be sadly to misunderstand its nature. It represented a striving, on the part of a class emerging from centuries of internecine warfare and economic stagnation, towards a mode of life adapted to a new-found leisure and the enjoyment of a certain culture till recently the apanage of clerks and clerics. The knight, no longer a warrior from the cradle to the grave, was forced to find some other means of occupying his time and justifying his existence, and the twin ideals of chivalry and *courtoisie* met all his needs. The service of Holy Church, of the weak and the defenceless, was a convenient vindication of his martial appetites, and idleness could be commuted into the self-perfectioning, not of the spiritual, but of the social man. Love was at once the mainspring and the goal of these redirected energies. Certainly the concept of feudal service provided the pattern on which the new relationship was built, but the imperious and disdainful lady subjecting her lover to her every whim is only one facet of the picture. In the widest sense any love was courtly that did not tend to the immediate satisfaction of physical desire (the emphasis being on the word immediate), and which acted as a spur to self-improvement. The degree of subjection on the lover's part was in direct relation to the unattainability of the lady (whether its cause was moral scruple or social position or both); the extent to which the passion was sublimated depended on individual sensibilities: for at its most etherealized this was a goal accessible only to an initiated élite. There were therefore almost as many variations on the theme as there were couples to interpret it. Hence at one extreme we have the lovers in *The Chatelaine of Vergy*, veritable virtuosos of the art; somewhere in the middle the couple in *The Lay of the Reflection* who appear to be playing a delightful if dangerous game over which they have more control than they would wish to admit; and at the other the charming but uncomplicated devotion of Aucassin and Nicolette, or Sir William and the high-born damsel he aspires to wed. In all four cases the relationship is courtly: the standpoint varies according to the plot and the idiosyncrasies of each particular author.

The Count of Pontieu's Daughter provides a contrast to the other tales and can in no sense be termed courtly. It is a much more primitive story, depending for its effect on an element of mystery not resolved until near the end. It is in its way a psychological drama, but its workings are never more than suggested and the whole story is imbued with an enigmatic quality that continues to intrigue. It doubtless appealed in its own day by the opportunities it offered for debating moral problems of some nicety, which had a perpetual fascination for the legalistic medieval mind.

Five tales, therefore, each truly of its time, but all capable of speaking to other times than theirs; and if it is true that one man's meat is often another man's poison, the fare, I hope, is varied enough to afford every palate a modicum of pleasure.

AUCASSIN AND NICOLETTE

Introduction

THE anonymous author of *Aucassin and Nicolette* calls his work a 'cantefable', in reference to its composite nature, part prose and part verse. Whether or not he coined the word to describe an art form of his own invention we do not know. Certainly no other Old French text features these alternating passages of prose and verse, and as for the Arabian romances which were once thought, no doubt erroneously, to have served as models for the French poet, their verse sections are purely lyrical in character, whereas in *Aucassin* they are woven into the chain of the narrative and carry the story along.

That the work has come down to us in a single manuscript, itself hastily copied by a slapdash scribe, seems to indicate a lack of popular appeal. But whether this was due to the unusual formula, or to the fact that the work fell uneasily between the romance on the one hand and the nascent secular drama on the other, is a moot point. Again, it may simply stem from the author's own reluctance to see rival entertainers cash in on his success. The work was plainly intended for public declamation: this much is proved by the embryonic stage-directions that head each passage, and we still have the tune to which the verse was sung. There has been much debate as to whether it was staged as a play, or merely delivered as a dramatic monologue. The general consensus tends towards the latter, seeing the work as a 'mime' for one or perhaps two players, dispensing with scenery and relying on voice and gesture for dramatic effect.

Of the author we know nothing except that he wrote in the dialect of northern France, probably during the first half of the thirteenth century, and would seem to have been a professional *jongleur*. This appears not only from the form he adopted for his tale, but from his easy familiarity with the literary conventions of his day, his use of the stock epithet, the formulated description, his fluent versifying and above all the marvellous skill with which he forged a highly distinctive and personal style out of the common-places of the minstrel's stock-in-trade. There is no reason to suppose that he knew the South of France, the setting for his story. Had he visited Provence he might have avoided having his hero ship-wrecked on the Rhône, beneath the walls of a town some thirty miles up-river; yet again he might not, so airy is his attitude to time and place.

That he was a gay, inconsequent and light-hearted fellow, with a keen eye for the ridiculous, and enough good sense and taste withal to ride his foolery on a tight rein is apparent from the only legacy he left posterity. This sparkling parody, at bottom an illustration of the adage that the path of true love never did run smooth, pokes gentle and good-humoured fun at every literary convention of its time, and in so doing runs through the entire gamut of comedy from delicate irony to the wildest farce.

It is the story of a love-lorn youth, one Aucassin by name, who yearns after an orphan girl brought up by one of his father's vassals. Being forbidden to marry her, or indeed speak to her, he, as it were, goes on strike – surely one of the earliest examples of the with-drawal of labour? He refuses to fight in his father's war against a rapacious neighbour and moons around the castle dreaming of Nicolette. When, in return for a promise that he will be able to ex-change a few sweet words with her, he boldly takes up arms and sallies forth to battle, his love for his fair one, that ought by all courtly standards to fire him with valour, zeal and fiercest hardi-hood, instead leaves him totally bemused, to be ignominiously taken prisoner by his foes. Only then, when the prospect of sudden death makes him realize that he will be deprived of Nicolette for ever, does he recover his wits and turn the tables on his enemies.

The rest of the story recounts the lovers' imprisonment and subsequent escape, their flight together and their various adventures, which include a visit to the Land of Topsy-Turvy, where Aucassin appears in a new role as the one sane man in a crazy world.

The story, in terms of action, is slight. It is the manner, not the matter, that counts. The author excels at painting scenes and ren-dering dialogue. There is a charming, and amusing, pastoral interlude when the lovers meet, singly, with a group of herd-boys in the forest, and again when Aucassin, weeping at having lost all trace of Nicolette, encounters a boorish but good-hearted ploughboy who mocks him for a milksop.

All the literary conventions and tricks of style are parodied in turn: the exaggerations of the courtly code for a start; and then the time-worn clichés of the epic in the two battle scenes, one fought with rotten apples. The verse sections are less marked by irony, and some have a genuine lyrical quality, but there are, too, the lines addressed by Aucassin to his lost love whom, by a flight of fancy, he chooses to identify with the evening star. He wishes he could fly aloft to join her, shrugging off the possible damage to be sustained on his return to earth; this from the bold knight who has just dislocated his shoulder falling off his horse which was *grand et haut*. Finally the series of adventures leading to the inevitable happy ending draw their comic effect from the technique of exaggeration. In a pastiche of the more far-fetched romances the author sets off at a gallop through the realm of the improbable, showing a blithe unconcern for those realistic touches which are supposed to sugar the pill of implausibility and make it easier to swallow. Thus, riding helter-skelter through the literary landscape, he brings his tale to a happy close and his lovers to their journey's end.

Light-hearted entertainment? Yes, assuredly. But *Aucassin and Nicolette* has an idyllic quality that makes it more than that and sets it in a class apart. Love itself is not mocked, only its more extravagant manifestations. The author's sympathy is with the lovers – indeed, according to him, even the Almighty loves a lover. He takes great care, too, to ensure that his hero never forfeits our amused affection. This he achieves partly by endowing him with a number of wholly admirable features: constancy, beauty, courage when the occasion demands it, tenderness and a quality of innocent amiability which is totally endearing; and partly by presenting him as the object of Nicolette's devotion. Now Nicolette is the most entrancing of figures. She must have broken as many hearts as Helen. Venerable scholars have succumbed to her charms. F. W. Bourdillon prefaced an edition with an ode to her. She is the real heroine of the story. While Aucassin weeps and dotes and wrings his hands,

Nicolette works for both of them; she schemes and plans, she comforts her lover and revives his flagging courage, she even offers to renounce him for his own good, she spurns a kingdom for his sake, and finally makes her own way back to him, disguised as a wandering minstrel, to see whether he loves her still. Feminine to the last, when she finds him still as fond and still as tearful, she keeps the secret of her identity until she has had time to wash and change and array herself more suitably. If such a paragon can find her happiness in Aucassin, who are we to quibble at his shortcomings? Let us accept with all tranquillity of mind the author's assurance that the lovers, having at last attained their bliss, lived happily ever after.

The Verse

The author adopted for his verse passages the epic *laisse* of irregular length, in assonance as opposed to rhyme. Unlike the epic line however which was, typically, decasyllabic, the line used here has seven syllables, except in the four sections (§3, §5, §33 and §37) where the lines end with an unstressed feminine 'e'. The final hemistich of each section is composed of four syllables only, not counting the feminine ending which appears in all. This metre was much favoured in popular songs and lyric poetry of the period.

I have, as far as I could, respected the verse form; but since in English metre is determined by stress rather than by syllable-count, I have felt justified in adding an initial unstressed syllable where this made the verse run more smoothly. In two stanzas I have also allowed myself a final unstressed syllable; in the first case, in §7, I found it impossible to render some of the lines otherwise; in the second, §21, it seemed the only way of conveying the deliberately naïve tone of the herd-boys' song, which the poet achieves by the repeated use of the diminutive '–et' as suffix (e.g. Aucassinet for Aucassin etc.).

The assonance posed a more difficult problem. F. W. Bourdillon, who brought out in 1897 an edition of the work with his own translation on the facing page, had this to say on the subject:

Among the Romance languages, in which the vowels are stronger than the consonants, assonance became fully established as an artistic method. In English, on the other hand, in which the consonant-sounds generally overpower or weaken the vowel-sounds, it never gained any footing. In fact English assonances are hardly perceptible except in a dissyllabic form, such as *harvest* and *farthest* . . . as to single assonances, I came to the conclusion that it was almost hopeless to try to use them in English as a poetic method, or to obtain from them the necessary effect of recurrent sounds, except by using rhymes as well.

It might be added that assonance is greatly facilitated in French by the grammatical structure of the language, in particular the similarity of verb endings. In point of fact Bourdillon opted, as has been the universal practice with this text as far as I am aware, for the rhyming couplet. Wishing however to keep as close as possible to the original form, I have retained a semblance of assonance, while taking certain liberties. That is to say that I have used in the same stanza vowel-sounds that are reasonably close without being identical (e.g. blood, lord, proud, etc.) and at times a mixture of i sounds and e sounds. At the same time, following Bourdillon's suggestion, I have reinforced the assonance with a fair sprinkling of rhymes introduced, not in a regular pattern, but as the possibility occurred, with particular attention to the closing lines of each section.

The Music

(I am greatly indebted to the Very Rev. P. E. L. Peacock, M.A., D.Mus., Warden of Greyfriars, for the following paragraphs and the modern notation.)

Just as the *chansons de geste* were intoned to an incantatory air, constantly repeated, so the verse passages of *Aucassin and Nicolette*, on the evidence of the manuscript, were intended to be sung to a recurrent melody. The formula however was slightly more elaborate in that it comprised two musical phrases as the setting for the seven-syllabled lines and a separate cadence for the final hemistich.

It would be quite wrong to suppose a modern rigidity to the performance of the music since it is clear in other cases that the music which has come down to us is often merely a framework upon which the singer improvised, or, if the verses did not allow any elaboration, at least the singer could choose which musical phrases to sing. Some of the sections in *Aucassin and Nicolette*, having an uneven number of lines, do not fit into the regular pattern of the music and scholars have been at pains to explain this away by various ingenious suggestions. The fact is that the medieval story-teller had *carte blanche* to handle the music as he thought fit, and would adapt and re-order during the performance, very much as folk singers will still do today.

What is clear is that the first musical phrase ends with an *ouverte* (non-final) cadence and the following phrase is *clos* (final). Whilst the theory that the first phrase would be sung once and the rest of the verses of that section would be sung to a repeated second phrase could be upheld according to the disposition of the musical phrases, it is extremely unlikely that this was done. The two phrases fit together naturally and logically and provide a much better musical vehicle for the words. The various difficulties of fitting in the text on special occasions is not worse than occurs in any other re-interpretation of medieval music. The following is the generally accepted rendering:

Qui vau - roit bon vers o - ïr   Del de - port du viel an - tif
De deux biax en - fans pe - tis   Ni - cho - lete et Au - cassins

Tant par est   dou - ce.

EDITIONS

C'est d'Aucasin et de Nicolete, a reproduction in photo-facsimile of the MS., by F. W. Bourdillon, Clarendon Press, 1896.

Aucassin and Nicolette, edited and translated by F. W. Bourdillon, second edition, London, 1897.

Aucassin et Nicolette, ed. H. Suchier, eighth edition, Paderborn, 1913.

Aucassin et Nicolete, ed. M. Roques, Classiques Français du Moyen Age, Paris, 1929; second edition, revised, 1954.

Aucassin et Nicolete, ed. F. W. Bourdillon, Manchester University Press, 1930.

This list is by no means exhaustive and contains only the most recent editions. The last four all have copious notes, glossaries, etc., and I have used all four where occasion arose, basing my translation primarily on the text printed by Roques and supplementing where necessary.

A comprehensive list of studies, articles, etc., up to 1954 will be found in M. Roques's revised second edition. To that I would only add 'La Parodie et le Pastiche dans Aucassin et Nicolette' by O. Jodogne, *Cahiers de l'association internationale des lettres françaises*, XII, 1960.

Aucassin and Nicolette

[1] Who would hear a goodly lay
   Of a dotard old and grey
   Parting fair young lovers twain,
   Aucassin and Nicolette;[1]
   Of the trials the youth did bear,
   Of the deeds of valour rare
   Compassed for his love so fair?
   Sweet the song and choice the tale,
   Well-ordered, and in courtly vein;
   There is no man in sore travail,
   Extreme of misery or pain,
   Or stricken with an illness grave
   But if he hear it will be healed,
   Restored again to joy and weal,
                    Such is its grace.

Here they say and tell and relate

[2] that Count Bolgar of Valence was engaged in a war against Count Garin of Beaucaire, a war so desperate, fierce and murderous that not a day dawned without finding him at the gates and walls and defences of the town with a hundred knights and ten thousand foot and horsemen; and meanwhile he burned and ravaged the land and killed Count Garin's men.

Count Garin of Beaucaire was old and feeble, a man who had outlived his time. He had no heir, male or female, save one youth whom I will describe to you. Aucassin was the young man's name, and he was handsome and comely and tall, with a fine figure, and legs, arms and feet to match it. He had fair and tightly curling hair, laughing grey eyes, a fresh complexion, and a high-bridged nose well set in an oval face. So well endowed was he with good qualities that there was never a bad one to be found in him; but he was so smitten by all-conquering love that he would neither be a knight, nor take up arms, nor go a-tourneying, nor do any of those things he ought.

His father and mother would say to him:

'Go to, son, take your arms and mount your horse and set about defending your land and helping your men. If they see you among them they will put up a better fight for their lives and chattels and for the land that is yours and ours.'

'Father,' replied Aucassin, 'what are you talking about? May God never grant me anything I ask Him, if ever I take up arms, or mount a horse, or go to do battle in the press where I might strike some knight or he me, unless you give me Nicolette, my own sweet love, whom I love so dearly.'

'Son,' said the father, 'that is out of the question. Leave Nicolette be: for she is a captive who was brought from foreign parts; the viscount of this town purchased her from the Saracens and brought her back and stood sponsor to her at her baptism; he brought her up as his godchild and will provide her one of these days with a young fellow who will earn her bread for her in honourable service. You have no call to meddle in this, and if it is a wife you want I will give you the daughter of a king or a count. There is no man in France, however great, whose daughter you may not have for the asking.'

'Tush! father,' said Aucassin, 'where is that earthly dignity that Nicolette, my own sweet love, would not enhance, if it were hers? Were she empress of Constantinople or of Germany, or queen of France or England it would be little enough for her, so filled is she with all good qualities and every grace that goes with gentle birth.'

Here it is sung.

[3] Aucassin was of Beaucaire,
    A castle pleasant, fine and fair.
    From the lissom Nicolette
    None could wean his heart away,
    Not though father said him nay
    And mother spoke with warning grave:[2]

'What would you do! Fie now, for shame!
Pretty she may be and gay:
From Carthage city[3] she's a waif,
Purchased from a pagan sheikh.
Since you seek the wedded state
Take a wife of high estate.'
'Mother, I will not be swayed.
In Nicole there is nothing base,
Svelte of body, fair of face –
My heart is lightened by her grace;
When she's so sweet, 'tis quite in place
     Her love to claim.'

Here they say and tell and relate.

[4] When Count Garin of Beaucaire saw that he would never manage to wean his son Aucassin from his love for Nicolette, he went to the viscount of the city, who was his vassal, and hailed him with the words:

'Sir viscount, you must get rid of your goddaughter Nicolette. A curse upon the land from which she was brought to this country! For now, on account of her, I am losing Aucassin, since he refuses to be a knight or do anything he ought. And let me tell you that if I hear any more of it I will burn her at the stake, and you will have good cause to fear for yourself as well.'

'Sir,' said the viscount, 'his comings and goings and parleyings I wholly deplore. I bought her with my money and stood sponsor to her at her baptism and made her my godchild, and intended providing her with a young fellow who would have earned her bread for her in honourable service. Your son Aucassin had no call to meddle in this. But since it is your will and your good pleasure, I will despatch her to a country so far distant that he will never set eyes on her again.'

'Look to it then,' retorted Count Garin. 'It could go ill with you else.'

With that they parted.

Now the viscount was a rich man and had a fine palace giving on-

to a garden. There he had Nicolette shut up in a room on an upper
storey with an old woman as associate and companion, and had them
furnished with bread and meat and wine and everything they needed.
Then he had the door sealed up so that there was no way in or
out, save that there was a narrow window on the garden side which
gave them a little air.

Here it is sung.

[5] Nicolette is in duress,
    In a vaulted room confined,
    Which art and cunning had combined
    To decorate in wondrous wise.
    At the window now she leaned,
    Resting on the marble sill;
    Her hair was bright with golden shine
    And delicate the eyebrow's line:
    Fair of feature, fresh of cheek,
    Never was such beauty seen!
    Looking to the woodland green
    She saw the full-blown eglantine,
    Heard birds singing each to each
    And felt her plight more bitter still.
    'Alas!' she cried, 'Poor wretch am I!
    Why am I in prison pent?
    Aucassin, my own sweet squire,
    All my love to you is given,
    You I know are fond of me;
    For you I'm under lock and key,
    In this vaulted room confined
    Where a weary life is mine,
    But, by Mary's Son divine,
    Here will I not long repine
        Of my free will.'

Here they say and tell and relate.

[6] Nicolette, as you have heard, was held captive in the chamber.

The rumour went abroad through all the land that she was lost. Some said she had fled the country, others averred that Count Garin of Beaucaire had had her murdered. If anyone rejoiced, it was not Aucassin; he went straight to the viscount of the city and hailed him with the words:

'Sir viscount, what have you done with Nicolette, my own sweet love, the person I loved best in all the world? Have you taken her from me and stolen her away? Let me tell you that if I die as a result of this, you will be made to pay for it,[4] and rightly so, for you will have killed me with your own two hands by taking from me that which I loved best in all the world.'

'Good sir,' said the viscount, 'leave this be. Nicolette is a captive whom I brought back from foreign parts and bought with my money from the Saracens. I stood sponsor to her at her baptism and brought her up as my godchild, and intended providing her one of these days with a young fellow who would have earned her bread for her in honourable service. You have no call to meddle in this; take instead the daughter of a king or a count. Besides which, what do you think you would have gained if you had made her your mistress or taken her to your bed? Precious little, for your soul would sojourn in hell for it till the end of time, for you'd never enter heaven.'

'What would I do in heaven? I have no wish to enter there, unless I have Nicolette, my own sweet love, whom I love so dearly. For to heaven go only such people as I'll tell you of: all those doddering priests and the halt and one-armed dotards who grovel all day and all night in front of the altars and in fusty crypts, and the folk garbed in rags and tatters and old, worn cloaks, who go barefoot and bare-buttocked and who die of hunger and thirst and cold and wretchedness. These are the ones who go to heaven, and I want nothing to do with them. Nay, I would go to hell; for to hell go the pretty clerks and the fine knights killed in tournaments and splendid wars, good soldiers and all free and noble men. I want to go along with these. And there too go the lovely ladies, gently bred and mannered, those who have had two lovers or three besides their lords, and there go gold and silver, and silk and sable,[5] and harpers and minstrels and all the kings of this world. I want to go along with these, provided I have Nicolette, my own sweet love, with me.'

'In truth,' said the viscount, 'it's no use your talking of her, for you will never see her again. And if you should speak to her, and your father heard of it, he would burn her and me at the stake and you would have good cause to fear for yourself as well.'

'It grieves me much,' said Aucassin. And he left the viscount, most disconsolate.

Here it is sung.

[7] Aucassin retraced his steps,
Most dejected and distressed.
No one can his sorrow mend
At having lost his pretty friend
Nor any helpful course suggest.
To the palace now he pressed,
Climbed the stairway step by step,
Then into a chamber went
Where he with woe and wild lament
And tears of sorrow freely shed
Began his dear one to regret:
'Nicolette, most sweet your presence,
Sweet at meeting, sweet at severance,
Sweet your converse and addresses,
Sweet your dalliance, sweet your jesting,
Sweet your kisses, sweet caresses,
For you I am with sorrow vexed
And with grief so sore beset
That I fear 'twill be my death,
Most dear, sweet friend.'

Here they say and tell and relate.

[8] While Aucassin was in the chamber bewailing the loss of his dearest Nicolette, Count Bolgar of Valence, who had his war to wage, did not neglect his duty; far from it, he had summoned his

horse and his footmen and now marched on the castle to attack it. The alarm was raised, the knights and soldiers armed and ran to the gates and walls to defend the castle, while the townspeople climbed to the ramparts and hurled down cobble-stones and sharpened stakes.

During the thick of the assault Count Garin of Beaucaire walked into the chamber where Aucassin was making lamentation and bewailing the loss of Nicolette, his own sweet love, whom he loved so dearly.

'Ah, son!' he cried, 'what a wretched and hapless plight is yours to see your very best and strongest castle under attack! And be sure that if it falls you lose your inheritance! Go to, son, take your arms and mount your horse and ride out into the battle to defend your land and help your men. Even if you never strike a knight nor are struck by one, so long as your men see you among them they will put up a better fight for their lives and chattels and for the land that is yours and mine. You are such a big, strapping lad that you can very well do it, and do it you ought.'

'Father,' said Aucassin, 'what are you talking about? May God never grant me anything I ask Him, if ever I take up arms, or mount a horse, or go to do battle in the press where I might strike some knight or he me, unless you give me Nicolette, my own sweet love, whom I love so dearly.'

'Son,' said his father, 'that is out of the question; I would sooner suffer the loss of my land and of all I have than see you take her to your wedded wife.'

He turned away. And when Aucassin saw him walking off he called him back.

'Father,' he called, 'come here. I will strike a good bargain with you.'

'What bargain, my good son?'

'I will take arms and go out to battle on the condition that, if God brings me back safe and sound, you will let me see Nicolette, my own sweet love, long enough for me to say two or three words to her and give her just one kiss.'

'Granted,' said his father.

He gave him his word and Aucassin was happy.

Here it is sung.

[9] Aucassin heard of the kiss
    That returning would be his;
    Not ten thousand golden pieces
    Could have filled him with such bliss.
    He demanded armour rich,
    'Twas made ready at his wish;
    He donned a mail shirt double-ringed,
    Laced the helm beneath his chin,
    Secured the sword with golden hilt,
    Mounted then his charger swift;
    Next he took his lance and shield,
    And glancing downwards at his feet
    Saw them both in stirrups fixed,
    Thought himself a paladin.
    Recalling then his love so sweet
    Suddenly he spurred his steed;
    Nothing loth, the charger fleet
    Headed for the gate full speed
        Where battle seethed.

Here they say and tell.

[10] Aucassin was now armed and mounted, as you have heard.
God almighty! how admirably did the shield hang from his neck,
the helm sit on his head and the sword-belt lie against his left side!
A tall, strong youth was he, handsome and comely and well-built,
the horse he sat on was swift and fleet, and the lad had headed him
straight for the gate. Now, do not imagine that he was intent on
seizing cattle or goats, or on giving or receiving blows. Not a bit of
it. Such matters never crossed his mind; instead he was thinking so
hard of Nicolette, his own sweet love, that he forgot his reins and
every single thing he ought to be doing. His charger, meanwhile,
stung by the spurs, galloped straight through the press and carried
him right into the midst of his foes. From all sides arms shot out

and seized him, his shield and lance were wrested from him and in a trice he was led away prisoner, with his captors already discussing how they would put him to death. When Aucassin heard what they were saying:

'Ah, God!' he cried, 'Sweet Lord Incarnate! Are these my mortal foes who are now leading me away and are about to cut off my head? And once my head is off I shall never again speak to Nicolette, my own sweet love, whom I love so dearly. I still have a good sword here and I am sitting on a good, fresh horse. If I do not defend myself now for her sake, may God never help her if she ever loves me more!'

The youth was tall and strong, and the horse he was riding was a mettlesome beast. He set his hand to his sword and began to smite to left and right, slicing through helms and nose-guards, wrists and arms, and laying murderously about him like the wild boar set upon by hounds in the forest, with the result that he unhorsed ten of their knights and wounded seven, before suddenly breaking loose from the scrimmage and galloping headlong back with sword held high.

Count Bolgar of Valence, having heard that his enemy Aucassin was to be hanged, was making his way across just then, and Aucassin did not fail to spot him. Gripping his sword, he dealt the other a blow which dented helm and head. The count was so stunned that he fell to the ground and Aucassin reached down and, grabbing hold of him, led him away prisoner by the nose-guard and delivered him up to his father.

'Father,' said Aucassin, 'here is your enemy who has harassed and wronged you so cruelly. This war has dragged on for twenty years without any man being able to put an end to it.'

'Good son,' replied the father, 'set about winning your spurs, instead of building castles in the air!'

'Father,' retorted Aucassin, 'don't preach to me, but keep your bargain.'

'Bah! what bargain, my boy?'

'Tush! father, have you forgotten it? Upon my oath, whoever else forgets it, I have no intention of doing so; on the contrary I have it greatly at heart. Did you not make a bargain with me, when I took arms and went into battle, that if God brought me back safe and sound you would let me see Nicolette, my own sweet love, long enough to say two or three words to her? And you promised me I should give her just one kiss, and that is the bargain I would have you keep.'

'I?' said his father. 'May God never help me if ever I keep such a bargain. If she were here now I would burn her at the stake and you would have good cause to fear for yourself as well.'

'Is that your last word?' asked Aucassin.

'So help me God,' said his father, 'it is.'

'In truth,' said Aucassin, 'I am most grieved to see a man of your age playing false. Count of Valence,' he added, 'you are my prisoner!'

'Indeed I am, sir,' said the count.

'Give me your hand,' said Aucassin.

'Sir, most gladly.'

And he placed his hand in Aucassin's.

'Pledge me this,' said Aucassin: 'while you live and are in a position to do my father injury or harm in respect of his person or goods, not to let a day pass without your doing it.'

'Sir, for God's sake, do not make fun of me, but put me to ransom. Whatever you ask, be it gold or silver, horses or palfreys, silk or sable, hounds or hawks, I will give it you.'

'What!' said Aucassin, 'do you not then admit that you are my prisoner?'

'Sir, indeed I do,' said Count Bolgar.

'Then may God never help me if I do not send your head flying, unless you pledge me this!'

'In God's name!' cried the other, 'I pledge you whatever you please.'

He gave him his pledge, and Aucassin had him mount a horse and he himself mounted another and escorted him to safety.

Here it is sung.

[11] When Count Garin grew aware
     That he ne'er would separate

Aucassin his son and heir
From the lovely Nicolette,
He put him into close restraint
In a subterranean gaol
Walled in marble dark and drear.
Here the youth knew such despair
As he'd never had to bear,
Started to bewail his fate
Most bitterly, as you shall hear.
'Nicole, as the lily fair,
Sweetest love, with mien so clear,
Sweeter are you than the grape,
Or than sop in mazer veined.[6]
A pilgrim I did see of late,
A traveller from Aquitaine,
Whom a reeling sickness ailed
And kept upon his pallet laid.
He was in a parlous state,
Stricken with an illness grave.
Passing close by where he lay
You happened to lift up your train,
Lifted too your ermine cape
And snow-white shift, and thus you bared
Your dainty ankle to his gaze.
Cured was he without delay,
Never had he been so hale,
Sprang up from his bed of pain,
Homeward hied him debonair,
Whole and healed and sound again.
Sweet love, as the lily fair,
You go and come in beauty rare.
Sweet in dalliance, sweet in play,
Sweet your talk and winsome ways,
Sweet to fondle and embrace,
No one could but hold you dear.
For you I lie imprisoned strait
In this subterranean gaol,

All alone to rant and rave,
Till this cell becomes my grave,
 For your sweet sake.'

Here they say and tell and relate.

[12] So Aucassin was imprisoned, as you have heard, and
Nicolette, in another part of the town, was in the vaulted room.
It was summer-time, and the month of May, when the days are long
and warm and bright and the nights calm and still. As Nicolette lay
one night in her bed, the sight of the bright moonlight pouring
through the window and the sound of the nightingale singing in the
garden put her in mind of Aucassin, her own true love, whom she
loved so dearly. She fell to thinking of Count Garin of Beaucaire
who hated her with a mortal hatred, and decided that she would not
stay any longer where she was: for if she were denounced and
Count Garin knew of it, he would have her cruelly put to death.
She sensed that the old woman who kept her company was asleep.
So she rose and put on a long tunic of good silk cloth that she had
with her, and took bedlinen and towels, which she knotted together
to form the longest rope she could, and having tied one end to the
mullion she slid down into the garden. Then kilting her clothing in
front and behind with either hand on account of the heavy dew she
saw on the grass, she slipped away down the garden.

 She had fair and tightly curling hair, laughing grey eyes, a straight
nose nicely set in an oval face, and red lips, brighter than any cherry
or rose in June; her teeth were small and white, and her small, firm
breasts lifted the bodice of her dress as they might have been two
walnuts, while her waist was so tiny that you could have ringed it
with your two hands; and the daisy heads she broke off with her
toes, and which bestrewed her insteps, looked downright black
against her feet and legs, so white was the young maid's skin.

 She came to the postern gate and opened it, and passed through
and out down the streets of Beaucaire, keeping to the shadow for the
moon was shining brightly, and went on her way till she came to
the tower where her lover lay. The masonry was fissured here and
there, so, flattening herself against one of the pillars with her cloak

pulled tight about her, she put her head in through a chink in the tower, which was old and ruinous, and there she heard Aucassin weeping within and making great lamentation, and regretting his own sweet love whom he loved so dearly. When she had heard enough she began to speak.

Here it is sung.

[13]   Fairest, loveliest Nicole,
      Huddled close against the wall,
      Heard her Aucassin distraught
      Weeping for the love he'd lost.
      Then in turn she spoke her thoughts:
      'Aucassin, so brave and bold,
      Noble youth of high renown,
      What avails you thus to mourn,
      Weep and wail and sigh and moan,
      When I never shall be yours?
      Your father hates me and abhors,
      Likewise do his kinsmen all.
      For love of you the sea I'll cross,
      Hie me to a foreign coast.'
      Cutting off some golden locks,
      She tossed them to her lover bold,
      Who upon this treasure trove
      Every reverence bestowed,
      Kisses and caresses showered,
      In his bosom safely stored,
      Then fell to weeping as before,
              For his dear love.

Here they say and tell and relate.

[14] When Aucassin heard Nicolette declare that she intended fleeing to another country he was far from pleased.

'Dear, sweet love,' he said, 'you shall not go, for it would be the death of me. And the first man who set eyes on you, and could make shift, would put you in his bed and make you his mistress. And once you had lain in any man's bed but mine, do not imagine that I should wait until I found a knife which I could plunge into my heart and so make an end of me. Nay truly, I should not wait that long, I should hurl myself at the first wall or block of granite that I saw and dash my head against it so hard that my eyeballs would start from their sockets and I would brain myself outright. I would sooner die that sort of a death than know you had lain in any man's bed but mine.'

'Ah!' replied Nicolette, 'I do not believe you love me as much as you say; on the contrary, I love you better than you do me.'

'Tush! my sweet love,' said Aucassin, 'it would be impossible for you to love me as much as I do you. Women cannot love men as much as men love women. For a woman's love resides in her eye, and in the nipple of her breast, and in her big toe, but a man's love is planted deep in his heart, whence there is no escaping.'

While Aucassin and Nicolette stood talking together, the watch was coming along the street. The men had drawn swords under their cloaks, for Count Garin had ordered them to kill the girl if they could catch her. The watchman high on the tower saw them coming and heard them talking of Nicolette and threatening to kill her.

'God!' he exclaimed, 'what a pity it would be if they killed so lovely a young maid! It would be a true work of mercy if I could warn her, unbeknownst to them, and she escaped them. For if they kill her it will be the death of my young lord, Aucassin, and that would be a shame indeed.'

Here it is sung.

[15]   The watchman was a gallant knave,
      Quick of wit, discreet and brave;
      In a trice he rived the air
      With a ditty sweet and clear:
      'Maid with noble heart and gay,
      Tender is your body's grace,
      Shining tresses golden fair,
      Eyes alight in laughing face.

Your demeanour tells me plain
That you've spoken with your swain
Who will soon for your dear sake
Go despairing to his death.
Now I warn you, so give ear:
Of the ruffians beware
Coming hotfoot on your trail,
Naked steel beneath each cape;
With fell intent they stalk the lane
And soon you'll suffer hurt and pain,
        Save you escape.'

Here they say and tell and relate.

[16] 'Hey!' cried Nicolette, 'may the souls of your father and mother repose in bliss for having given me so kind and courteous a warning! Please God, I will guard me well from them, and may God guard me from them too!'

Wrapping herself in her cloak, she pressed back into the shadow of the pillar until they had passed by, and then she took leave of Aucassin and went on her way till she came to the outer wall of the fortress. The wall had been breached and was patched up with wattle, and she clambered up and over till she found herself between the wall and the ditch. There she looked down and trembled to see how deep and how precipitous it was.

'Ah, God!' she exclaimed, 'Sweet Lord Incarnate! If I let myself fall I shall break my neck, and if I stay where I am I shall be caught tomorrow and burned at the stake. I had still sooner die here, though, than have all the populace gape at me tomorrow.'

Making the sign of the cross on her forehead she let herself slide down the ditch. When she got to the bottom her dainty feet and hands, which were not used to harsh treatment, were torn and scratched, and blood was running in at least a dozen places; she was so frightened, though, that she felt neither pain nor hurt. If getting into the ditch had been hard for her, getting out proved harder still. Having bethought herself that this was no place to stay, she found a sharpened stake that the townsfolk had hurled down during their defence of the castle, and setting one foot in front of the other, she struggled up till she came at last to the top.

At a distance of two bowshots lay the forest, which stretched for thirty good leagues in either direction and harboured wild beasts and divers kinds of snakes. She was afraid that if she penetrated its fastness these would kill her, and then again she thought that, should she be found where she was, she would be taken back to the town to be burned.

Here it is sung.

[17] Fairest, loveliest Nicole,
    Having scrambled up the moat,
    Started to bewail her lot
    And on Jesus Christ to call:
    'King of Glory, Lord of Lords!
    Now I know not where to turn.
    If I flee into the wood
    I shall fall a prey to wolves,
    To the lions and wild boars
    Prowling there in horrid hordes.
    If I wait till day return,
    Showing where I'm to be found,
    Soon the pyre will fiercely glow
    Where my body's to be burned.
    But, by that same Lord of Lords,
    I'd far sooner be devoured
    By wolf or lion or savage boar
    Than venture in the town once more
                   On any score!'

Here they say and tell and relate.

[18] Nicolette bewailed her fate most bitterly, as you have heard. Then she commended herself to God and went on her way till she found herself in the forest. She dared not penetrate very far on account of the wild beasts and snakes, so she snuggled down in a

dense thicket, and feeling drowsy, fell asleep. There she slept until well past prime,[7] at which hour the herd-boys sallied out of the town and turned their animals loose between the woods and the river. Forgathering then round a beautiful, clear spring which welled up close to the forest's edge, they spread out a cloak and placed their bread on it. While they were eating, Nicolette was awakened by the birdsong and the herd-boys' voices and came out on them suddenly.

'Good lads,' she said, 'the Lord God be your aid!'

'God bless you, too!' answered one who was readier with his tongue than the rest.

'Good lads,' she continued, 'do you know Aucassin, the son of Count Garin of Beaucaire?'

'Yes, we know him well.'

'Then so help you God, good lads,' said Nicolette, 'tell him there is a beast in this forest, and he is to come and hunt it; and if he can catch it there's not one limb of it that he would cede for a hundred gold marks, no, nor for five hundred, nor for any sum whatever.'

The herd-boys stared at her and were troubled by her beauty.

'Me tell him that?' said the one who had a readier tongue than the rest. 'A curse upon whoever speaks of it or whoever tells him that! What you say is moonshine; for in all this forest there's no beast, be it stag or lion or boar, so valuable that one of its quarters would fetch more than two pence, or three at the most, and you talk of such riches! God's curse upon whoever believes you or tells him such a story! You are a fay, and we do not fancy your company, so be on your way!'

'Ah, good lads,' she said, 'indeed you will tell him! This beast has a healing power which will cure Aucassin of his wound. And I have five shillings here in my purse, so take them and give him my message. And he has three days in which to hunt it, and if he does not find it within that time he will never be cured of his wound.'

'In faith,' said the other, 'we'll take the money, and if he comes this way we will tell him, but we won't go looking for him.'

'So be it,' she said, and taking her leave of the herd-boys she went on her way.

Here it is sung.

[19] Nicolette, so fair of mien,
From the herd-boys turned aside,
Set off through the forest green
Down a leafy woodland ride
Trod by folk in ancient times;
At a cross-roads she arrived
Where seven paths on seven sides
Stretched as far as eye could see.
There a fancy took her mind
Her lover Aucassin to try,
If he cared for her indeed
And loved her as he said he did.
So she gathered lilies bright,
And plucking herbs and fronds and leaves
That grow upon those scrublands wild,[8]
She made an arbour all entwined,
The fairest bower that e'er was seen.
Then she swore by God on high
If Aucassin came riding by
And did not rest his limbs awhile
For love of her beneath its eaves,
He should ne'er her lover be
      Nor his love she.

Here they say and tell and relate.

[20] Now Nicolette, as you have heard, had made this pretty
and delightful bower, and when she had interwoven it closely both
outside and in with flowers and leaves, she hid herself close by in a
thick bush to see what Aucassin would do. Meanwhile the rumour
spread abroad through all the land that Nicolette was lost. Some said
that she had fled, while others averred that Count Garin had had her
murdered. If anyone rejoiced at the news, Aucassin did not. His
father, Count Garin, had him released from prison and summoned

the local knights and maidens too, and arranged a splendid feast, thinking to cheer his son's spirits. While the revelling was at its height Aucassin stood leaning against a balustrade, most melancholy and downcast. Whoever else might be making merry, Aucassin had no desire to do so, seeing there was no sign of her he loved. A knight, observing him, went over and addressed him.

'Aucassin,' he said, 'I have suffered myself from the same malady that now ails you. If you care to trust me, I will give you some good advice.'

'Sir,' said Aucassin, 'thank you kindly. I should value some good advice.'

'Get on a horse,' said the other, 'and go and disport yourself in the forest yonder. You will see all the flowers and greenery and hear the birds singing. For aught one knows you may hear something to your advantage.'

'Sir,' said Aucassin, 'my heartfelt thanks. That will I do.'

He slipped out of the hall and hurried down the steps and across to the stable where his horse was kept. He had it saddled and bridled, and setting his foot in the stirrup, mounted and left the castle. He rode as far as the forest and on again till, coming at mid afternoon to the spring, he found the herd-boys with a cloak spread out on the grass eating their bread and making very merry.

Here it is sung.

[21]   See assembled herd-boys jolly,
        Martin, Aymar and young Johnny,
        Robin, Fruëlin and Aubrey.
        Quoth one lad: 'Companions merry,
        God help Aucassin right early,
        He's a fine youth, say I truly!
        And the maid with fitted bodice,
        She whose hair was gold and glossy,
        Eye so bright and face so bonny,
        And who gave us of her pennies
        For to buy us cakes in plenty,
        Knives and sheaths and good knobkerries,

Flutes and pipes that tweedle shrilly,
Horns that tootle. God-a-mighty
Keep the lassie!'

Here they say and tell and relate.

[22] On hearing the herd-boys Aucassin was put in mind of
Nicolette, his own sweet love whom he loved so dearly, and he
thought to himself that she had passed that way; so he clapped his
spurs to his horse's sides and approached the group.

'Good lads, God be your aid!'

'God bless you, too!' said the one who had a readier tongue than
the rest.

'Good lads, do repeat the song you were singing just now.'

'That we won't!' retorted the fellow who had a readier tongue
than the rest. 'A curse on anyone who sings it for you, good sir!'

'Good lads,' said Aucassin, 'do you not know me then?'

'Oh yes, we knew you well enough for Aucassin, our master's
son; we are the count's men, though, not yours.'

'Good lads, I pray you sing it.'

'Listen, odsblood!' replied the other. 'Why should I sing for
you if it didn't suit me too? When there's never a baron in this
land, barring Count Garin himself, if he found my oxen, cows or
sheep in his meadows or in his corn, who durst be so bold as to
chase them out, no, not to save his eyes from being put out, he
wouldn't. So why should I sing for you if it didn't suit me to?'

'If God be your aid, good fellow, you will indeed! Here, take
ten shillings that I have here in my purse.'

'Sir, we'll take the money, but I'll not sing for you, for I've taken
an oath on it. But I'll tell it you if you like.'

'So be it!' said Aucassin, 'I'd sooner have telling than nothing.'

'Well, sir, we were here earlier on between prime and terce,
and we were eating our bread by this spring, just as we are now,
and a maid came up, the fairest thing on earth, so lovely that we
thought she was a fay, and the whole wood was a-dazzle with the
beauty of her; and she gave us money enough for us to promise her
that if you came this way we would tell you to go hunting in the

43

forest: for there's a beast within, which, so be you could catch it, you'd not give a single limb of for five hundred silver marks, nor for any sum whatever. For this beast has a healing power which will cure you, so be you can catch it, of your wound; and you have three days to catch it in, and if you haven't caught it by then you will never see it again. So hunt it if you wish, and leave it if you don't, for I have kept my part of the bargain.'

'Good lad,' said Aucassin, 'you have said quite enough. God grant me now to find it!'

Here it is sung.

[23] Aucassin heard every word
    Spoken by his lissom love
    And his heart was deeply moved.
    Hastily his leave he took,
    Headed deep into the wood;
    Swiftly did his pounding horse
    Carry him through brake and copse.
    As he rode he spoke his thoughts:
    'Nicolette, my lissom love,
    For you the forest paths I rove,
    Hunting neither stag nor boar,
    Following no tracks but yours.
    Your bright eyes, your graceful form,
    Merry smile and sweet discourse
    Have pierced my heart with mortal wound.
    So it please almighty God
    I shall see you yet anon,
        My sweet, my own.'

Here they say and tell and relate.

[24] Aucassin kept up his headlong gallop through the forest, following one track after another. And don't imagine that the thorns and brambles spared him! Not a bit of it. They ripped his clothes till

44

the least torn could scarce have been mended, and blood was running from his arms and flanks and legs in thirty or forty places, so that one could have followed his trail by the blood that spattered the grass. But he was thinking so hard of Nicolette, his own sweet love, that he felt neither pain nor hurt, and thus he rode all day long through the forest without getting any word of her. When he saw evening drawing in and had not found her he began to weep.

He was riding along an old, grassy track when, looking ahead, he saw in his path a fellow whom I will describe to you. He was tall and weird and alarmingly ugly. He had a great mop of a head as black as smut with eyes set a palm's width apart, broad cheeks, an enormous flat nose with cavernous nostrils, thick lips redder than underdone meat and great ugly, yellow teeth. He was dressed in ox-hide boots and leggings laced with bast up to the knee, had a cloak draped about him which had two wrong sides, and was leaning on a great quarter-staff. Aucassin came on him suddenly and had a great fright when he saw him.

'Good friend, God be with you!'

'And God bless you!' said the other.

'So help you God, what are you doing here?'

'And what's that to you?' inquired the youth.

'Oh, nothing,' said Aucassin, 'I meant no harm, I assure you.'

'Why are you crying,' asked the other, 'and making such a hullabaloo? I'm sure if I was as rich as you the whole world couldn't make me cry.'

'Huh! do you know me then?' asked Aucassin.

'Yes, I know well enough that you are Aucassin, the count's son, and if you tell me why you are crying I will tell you what I am doing here.'

'Indeed,' said Aucassin, 'I will gladly tell you that. I came this morning to hunt here in the forest, and I had a white greyhound, there wasn't a finer anywhere, and I've lost it, and that is why I weep.'

'Listen to that!' said the other, 'by Our Lord's heart of flesh! To think that you were weeping for a stinking cur! God's own curse on the man who ever thinks well of you again, when there's not a baron in this land, however great, who wouldn't gladly give your father fifteen or twenty for the asking, and count himself happy to boot. Me, I could well weep and make a hullabaloo.'

'You? Why so, friend?'

'Sir, I will tell you why. I was hireling to a rich bondman and I guided his plough, and there were four oxen to it. Now three days ago I had a real piece of bad luck in that I lost the best of my oxen, Brownie, the pick of my team, and I'm looking for him now. I've had nothing to eat or drink for three days and I daren't go back to the town; for I should be thrown into prison since I haven't the wherewithal to pay for the animal. Out of all the wealth in Christendom I've nothing but what I stand up in. I had a poor mother who had nothing but a pallet, and that they dragged from under her, so that she lies on the bare straw, and I'm more grieved for her than for myself. For riches come and go; if I've lost this time I'll win another, and I'll pay off my ox when I can, and you won't find me crying on that score. And you were crying over a filthy cur! God's own curse on the man who ever thinks well of you again!'

'Truly, you are of good cheer, friend. Blessings on you! And what was your ox worth?'

'Sir, they're asking twenty shillings for it. I can't beat them down by a halfpenny.'

'Here,' said Aucassin, 'take these twenty shillings that I have in my purse and pay off your ox.'

'Sir,' he said, 'thank you kindly, and may God grant you to find what you seek!'

He walked away and Aucassin rode on. The night was clear and still, and he pursued his course till he came [to the place where the seven paths meet,] and [looking ahead he saw the bower which] Nicolette [had made. The bower was decked] and roofed with flowers both without, within and before, and nothing could have been more beautiful.[9] When Aucassin caught sight of it he pulled up short; and a shaft of moonlight was streaming into it.

'Ah! God,' he exclaimed, 'Nicolette, my own sweet love, was here, and she made this with her own fair hands. For the love of her and for her sweetness' sake, here will I now dismount and rest for the remainder of the night.'

He slipped his foot from the stirrup to dismount; now the horse was a great tall beast, and Aucassin was thinking so hard of Nicolette that he fell heavily on a stone and put his shoulder out. It hurt him badly, but he struggled as best he could, and having tied his horse with his other hand to a thornbush, he turned himself on his side and wriggled along till he was lying flat on his back in the arbour. Gazing up through a gap in the foliage he saw the stars in the sky above, and observing one that was brighter than the others he started to address it.

Here it is sung.

[25] 'Little star, I see you shine,
    Drawn towards the orb of night;
    Nicole is with you on high,
    My sweet love with tresses bright.
    Methinks God wants her in the sky
    To be a [light at eventide
    And shed more lustre on the night.
    Sweetest love, 'twere my delight
    Up the heavenly stair to climb,]
    Careless how I'd downward dive
    Could I but reach you on high.
    How I'd kiss and hug you tight!
    Though I came of royal line
    You would be a fitting bride,
        Most sweet love mine!'[10]

Here they say and tell and relate.

[26] Nicolette, on hearing Aucassin, came out to him, for she was close at hand. Entering the arbour, she threw her arms around his neck, and kissed and embraced him.

'Well found, dear sweet love!'

'And you, too, dear sweet love, well found!'

They kissed and hugged one another, and their joy was full.

'Ah! sweet love,' said Aucassin, 'my shoulder was badly hurt a moment since, but now that I have you I feel neither ache nor pain.'

Running her hands over him, Nicolette found that his shoulder was dislocated. She manipulated and kneaded it so skilfully with her white hands (God, who loves lovers, availing), that it went back into its socket. Then, taking flowers and fresh grass and green leaves, she made him a poultice with a strip of her shift, and he was completely healed.

'Aucassin, dear sweet love,' she said, 'bethink yourself what you will do. If your father has this forest searched tomorrow and I am found, whatever may happen to you, I shall be put to death.'

'Truly, dear sweet love, that would break my heart. But you will never fall into their hands if I can help it.'

So saying he mounted his horse and set his love in front of him, kissing and embracing her the while, and thus they took to the open country.

Here it is sung.

[27] Aucassin, true lover fond,
Noble, comely, fresh and blond,
From the forest fastness rode,
Nicole on his saddle-bow
In his arms enfolded close.
Tenderly he kissed her brow
And her eyes and chin and mouth,
Till she said in sober mood:
'Aucassin, my own dear love,
To what country are we bound?'
'Sweetest love, what do I know?
I care not where we may go,
Desert, wilderness or wood,
If only I can be with you.'
On they roved by dale and down
Thorough villages and towns,
To the coast they came at morn,
Alighting on the sandy floor
        By the sea shore.

Here they say and tell and relate.

[28] Now, as you have heard, the lovers had both dismounted, and taking his horse by the rein and his dear one by the hand Aucassin started to walk along the strand. [As he looked out to sea he sighted a merchant ship sailing close inshore.][11] He hailed the mariners who steered towards him and agreed, after some persuasion on his part, to take the lovers on board. When they were well out to sea a fierce and terrible storm got up, which blew them past country after country until they arrived off a foreign coast and sailed into the harbour of the castle of Topsy-Turvy.[12] They asked whose land they were come to and were told it belonged to the king of Topsy-Turvy. Aucassin next inquired what sort of a man he was and whether he had any war on hand.

'Yes, indeed,' they said, 'a most desperate.'

He took his leave of the merchants who commended him to God. Then he mounted his horse and with his sword at his side and his love before him, rode as far as the castle. There he asked where the king was to be found and was told that he lay in childbed.

'And where is his wife, then?'

She had taken the field, they told him, at the head of every man jack of the country. Aucassin was dumbfounded by this information; he rode on to the palace where he and his love alighted. While she held his horse, he, with his sword girded about him, mounted the steps and made his way to the chamber where the king was lying.

Here it is sung.

[29]   Aucassin of high descent
         To the royal chamber went
         Where the monarch lay in bed,
         At the couch's foot stopped dead
         And harangued the occupant.
         Listen now to what he said:
         'Go to, knave! Why liest abed?'
         Quoth the king: 'A son I've bred.
         When my thirty days are sped

49

And my vigour I regain,
Off to mass I will me get,
As my sire did in his reign,
And then my war incontinent
Against my foes malevolent
I'll wage again!' [13]

Here they say and tell and relate.

[30] When Aucassin heard the king speak in that fashion, he seized all the bedclothes covering him and flung them across the room. Behind him he spied a stick. He snatched it up, wheeled round and lashed out, drubbing the monarch so furiously that he ought by rights to have killed him.

'Ah! good sir,' cried the king, 'what do you want of me? Have you gone out of your wits that you beat me in my own house?'

'By God Incarnate!' shouted Aucassin, 'you wretched whoreson! I'll kill you unless you swear to me that no man in your land will ever lie in childbed again!'

The king swore to it, and when he had given his word:

'Sir,' said Aucassin, 'take me now where your wife is captaining the army.'

'Gladly, sir,' said the king.

He mounted his horse and Aucassin did the same, while Nicolette stayed behind in the queen's chambers. The king and Aucassin rode on their way till they came where the queen was, and found that the battle was being fought with rotten crab-apples and eggs and fresh cheeses. As Aucassin began to watch he was overcome with amazement.

Here it is sung.

[31] Aucassin reined in his horse;
Leaning on his saddle-bow
He began to look around
At that desperate battle-ground.
The warriors had laid in a store
Of fresh-made cheeses by the mound,

And big field-mushrooms, large and round,
And rotten crab-apples galore.
Who muddied most the river fords
Won the crown and the applause.
Aucassin so brave and proud
Watched awhile, then at that crowd
     He laughed aloud.

Here they say and tell and relate.

[32] Having viewed this extraordinary spectacle, Aucassin rode across to the king and spoke to him:

'Sir,' he asked, 'are these your enemies?'

'Yes, sir,' said the king.

'Would you like me to settle your accounts with them?'

'I would indeed.'

Aucassin put his hand to his sword and hurled himself into their midst, and began to smite to right and left, slaying a good number. When the king saw that he was killing them, he seized him by the bridle, shouting:

'Ah! good sir, you mustn't go killing them like that!'

'What?' said Aucassin, 'do you want me to avenge you or not?'

'Sir,' said the king, 'you have already overdone it. It is not our custom here to kill each other.'

While the enemy took to his heels Aucassin and the king returned to the castle of Topsy-Turvy. The local barons advised the king to drive Aucassin out of the country and keep Nicolette for his son, for she had every appearance of being nobly bred. Nicolette overheard this talk, and far from pleased, she spoke her mind.

Here it is sung.

[33] Said fair Nicolette: 'Sir king
  Of Topsy-Turvy, it would seem
  Your people think me mad indeed!
  When my lover fondles me,
  Soft and warm to hands and lips,

Then my mood attains such bliss
That not for any dance or jig,
Strain of harp or violin,
Game of hazard or of skill,[14]
    Care I a fig.'

Here they say and tell and relate.

[34] Aucassin knew great happiness and ease at the castle of
Topsy-Turvy, since he had the company of Nicolette, his own
sweet love, whom he loved so dearly. And while he was thus en-
joying his heart's ease a Saracen fleet came sailing up and attacked
the castle and took it by storm. They seized the treasure and carried
off men and women captive, Nicolette and Aucassin among them.
Aucassin was bound hand and foot and thrown into one ship and
Nicolette into another. Once out at sea there blew up a storm which
separated them. The ship in which Aucassin lay was blown so far off
course that it finally foundered beneath the castle of Beaucaire and
the inhabitants, who came running down to claim flotsam and jet-
sam, discovered Aucassin and recognized him. The people of
Beaucaire were overjoyed to see their young lord again, for Aucas-
sin had tarried three whole years at the castle of Topsy-Turvy, and
his father and mother had died in the interval. They escorted him up
to the castle where all swore fealty to him, and he governed his land
in peace.

Here it is sung.

[35] Thus did Aucassin repair
To his city of Beaucaire;
He ruled his country and his realm
In tranquillity and calm.
Yet swore he by the God of grace
That he was more disconsolate
For losing his fair Nicolette,
Than should he peradventure hear
That all his kin had met their death.
'Sweetest love, so fair of face,

52

Where you are I've no idea;
God did ne'er the realm create
Where I would not seek you straight
By land or sea, were I aware
        That you were there.'

Here they say and tell and relate.

[36] Here will we leave Aucassin and tell of Nicolette. The ship in which Nicolette found herself belonged to the king of Carthage, and he was in fact her father, and she had twelve brothers, all of them kings or princes. When they saw how beautiful she was, they rendered her every honour and paid court to her, and asked her repeatedly who she was, for she had every appearance of being nobly born and bred. But she was unable to tell them who she was, for she had been taken captive in infancy. So they sailed on their way till they came to the city of Carthage. And when Nicolette saw the castle walls and the country round, she knew where she was and recognized it for the land where she had been reared and taken captive as a little child, yet old enough for her to be certain now that she had once been the king's daughter and reared in the city of Carthage.

Here it is sung.

[37] Valiant, virtuous Nicole
    Found herself beside the shore,
    Saw the mansions and the walls,
    Splendid palaces and halls,
    And her hapless fate deplored.
    'Alas! that I was nobly born,
    Daughter of a monarch proud
    – Carthage city's sovereign lord –
    And cousin to the sultan too;
    Now I'm with a savage horde.
    Aucassin, so good and bold,
    I'm tormented by your love,
    It wrings my heart and fires my blood.

53

God grant me this, the Three in One,
To hold you in my arms once more
And feel again on face and mouth
The kisses which will slake my drouth,
                    My own dear lord!'

Here they say and tell and relate.

[38] When the king of Carthage overheard what Nicolette was saying he threw his arms about her neck.

'Most fair, sweet maid,' he exclaimed, 'stand in no awe of me but tell me who you are.'

'Sir,' she answered, 'I am the daughter of the king of Carthage and was abducted as a little child, it must be fifteen years ago.'

Her words convinced them that she spoke the truth, and they fêted her and escorted her to the palace with all the honours due to a king's daughter. They would have given her a pagan king to husband, but Nicolette had no mind to wed. She was there three or four days, devising some stratagem whereby she might go in search of Aucassin. She procured a viol and taught herself to play it; until one day they sought to marry her to a powerful pagan king; so she slipped away in the night and went down to the harbour where she sought refuge with a poor woman on the waterfront. She rubbed her head and face with a herb, staining her skin a swarthy shade. Next she had cloak, smock, shirt and breeches made, and fitted herself out to look like a wandering minstrel; then taking her viol she approached a mariner and prevailed on him to take her on board his ship. The sail was hoisted and after many days on the high seas they landed on the coast of Provence. There Nicolette disembarked, and taking her viol she played her way across the country till she came to the castle of Beaucaire where Aucassin then was.

Here it is sung.

[39]   Beneath the tower at Beaucaire
         Was Aucassin upon a day;
         Sat him on the palace stair

Amid his barons bold and brave.
The sight of flower and herb and spray,
The sound of birdsong in the air
Set him yearning once again
For his gallant Nicolette
Whom he'd loved for many a year
And now recalled with sighs and tears.
But lo! there stood she on the steps,
Took out her viol, her bow as well,
And straightway made her matter plain:
'Noble lords, give me your ear,
Be you seated far or near!
Would you like to hear a lay
Of Aucassin, a baron brave,
And Nicolette whom nought dismayed?
They loved with such a lasting flame
He sought her in the forest's maze;
In Topsy-Turvy's citadel
Pagans captured them one day.
We know not what the youth befell,
But Nicolette, the valiant maid,
In the keep at Carthage dwells,
For her father loves her well
Who's lord and king of that domain.
His councillors would have her wed
A pagan monarch false and fell.
Nicole holds him in disdain
For she loves a noble swain
Called Aucassin – the very same,
And swears by God's most hóly name
That she'll have no other mate
Than the youth for whom she aches
              With longing great.'

Here they say and tell and relate.

[40] When Aucassin heard the gist of Nicolette's song his spirits
soared, and he drew her aside and asked:

'Good friend, do you know anything of this Nicolette whom you were singing about just now?'

'Yes, sir, I know her for the best and finest and noblest creature that ever lived; she is daughter to the king of Carthage, who seized her in the raid in which Aucassin was captured, and was bearing her off to his city of Carthage when he discovered she was his daughter and welcomed her back with great rejoicing. They press her daily to marry one of the greatest kings in the whole of Spain. But sooner than wed, she would see herself hanged or burned at the stake, however great her suitor.'

'Ah! good friend,' said Count Aucassin, 'if you were willing to go back to that land and tell her to come and see me, I would give you as much of my wealth as you could venture to ask for or carry away. And be it known to you that for love of her I will not take a wife, no, not of the highest rank; I intend to wait for Nicolette and will have no wife but her. And had I known earlier where to find her, she would not be still to seek.'

'Sir,' replied Nicolette, 'if you were to do that, I would go and fetch her for your sake and for hers, for I love her dearly.'

He gave his solemn pledge and had twenty pounds paid out to her. As she left, he was weeping at the thought of Nicolette's sweet and tender ways; seeing his tears she said:

'Sir, do not lose heart: it will not be long before I bring her to this town and you see her with your own eyes.'

These words made him happy again, and Nicolette left him and went off down the town to the house of the viscountess, her godfather the viscount being dead. She took lodging there and in the course of conversation she poured out her story to the viscountess, who recognized her and knew her without doubt for the same Nicolette whom she had raised; whereupon she had her washed and bathed and kept her there a full week. Nicolette meanwhile anointed herself with a herb known as celandine[15] and recovered every jot of her former beauty. Next she attired herself in clothes of costly silk, of which her hostess had enough and to spare, and having seated herself in the chamber on a cushion of quilted silk, she called to the viscountess and bade her go for her lover Aucassin, which the lady did. On arriving at the palace she found Aucassin weeping and repining because Nicolette his love was so long a-coming. The lady called to him, saying:

'Aucassin, leave your lamentation and come along with me, and I will show you the thing which you love most in all the world: for it's Nicolette, your own sweet love, who has come from far-off lands to seek you out.'

And Aucassin was happy once again.

Here it is sung.

[41] Now when Aucassin heard say
  That his lovely Nicolette
  Was come again to his domain
  Joy he knew, was ne'er so great.
  Following in the lady's wake
  He hied him to the house in haste:
  To the chamber they repaired
  Where his loved one sat in wait.
  Ne'er knew Nicole joy so great
  As when she now beheld her swain
  And sprang to greet him from her seat.
  When Aucassin beheld his dear
  He reached for her with arms outspread,
  And folding her in fond embrace
  Tenderly kissed eyes and face.
  Apart that night the lovers lay,
  But shortly after break of day
  Aucassin his love did take
  To wife and lady of Beaucaire.
  They lived and loved for many a year
  And of sweet dalliance took their share.
  Now Aucassin and Nicolette
  Have all their joy: and so this lay
  Marks the end of song and tale,
     No more's to say.

THE LAY OF THE REFLECTION

Introduction

THIS charming poem was first published in 1836 in a collection of *lais* edited by Francisque Michel. The author had obligingly left his signature in the closing verses, but little more was known of him until the last years of the century when two longer works, the *Roman de l'Escoufle* and the *Roman de la Rose*, more commonly called *Guillaume de Dôle* to distinguish it from the more celebrated work of the same name, were published in quick succession. Comparison of the three enabled scholars to establish their common authorship and the case was finally proven by the discovery of Renart's name concealed in an anagram in the epilogue to each of the two romances.

No more is known of him than can be deduced from his works. He enjoyed the favour of two noble patrons: Baudouin VI, Count of Hainault, who took part in the Fourth Crusade and became in 1204 Emperor of Constantinople; and later Miles of Nanteuil who was elected in 1221 to the bishopric of Beauvais, and at whose behest this work would seem to have been written. No doubt he occupied some minor post about the court of these, or of some other lord. It has been inferred from the general tone of his works that he was a man of humble origins whose evident abilities and ready wit rendered him *persona grata* with the great. Certainly good fortune was his chosen recipe for success in life, and yet, to judge by the two poems *Du Plait Renart de Dammartin contre Vairon son Roncin* and *De Renart et de Piaudoue*, which have been attributed to his 'undignified but spirited old age', Fortune seems to have been a fickle mistress, neglecting the needs of her ageing votary.

One hopes that she deigned to look his way again before it was too late, for he was a man of much originality whose works do not appear to have met with the success they merited. There is but a single copy of each of his two romances, though the seven surviving manuscripts of *The Lay of the Reflection* point to a greater popularity in its case. His distinguishing characteristic as a writer was his realism. There is no trace of the exotic in his works. He is a master at describing the contemporary landscape, whether it be the castle or the tavern, the workshop or the tournament. He is also an artist in the use of dialogue; rhetoric is replaced by repartee, set speeches by the normal cut and thrust of conversation. He can even handle the monologue, that stumbling block of every medieval poet who saw in it a heaven-sent opportunity for displaying his clerkly training.

Nowhere does his mastery of direct speech appear to better advantage than in this tale. The story is of the slightest. A certain knight who, while enjoying an immoderate success with the opposite sex, has himself remained heart-whole and fancy-free, finally falls in love with the very non-pareil of womanhood. The lady is not only beautiful, she is too astute to succumb to a few blandishments, and has wit enough to hold her own against any suitor, however ardent. How shall he win her over? Since it would be a pity to spoil so good a story, suffice it to say that the tale begins, once the poet has introduced his hero, with the latter's decision to pay the lady a visit and try his luck. It ends, after a diversionary tactic or two, with the knight's triumph over the lady's scruples (more politic than moral). The intervening pages relate the battle of wits that takes place between them, he respectful, enamoured, pressing his case, she by turns politely mocking, scandalized, or wishing to appear so, hurt and resentful when she thinks she has been toyed with, but ever more tightly caught in the web of flattery that his infatuation spins about her.

It is a most polished piece of work, and one that only an acute observer of human nature could have written. It is neat, and witty, and thoroughly worldly. Which brings us back to the question touched on in the introduction: is it 'courtly'? To that one must answer: yes, it is, within its limits and with certain reservations. Jean Renart gives one the impression of a man completely conversant with the courtly code, using its vocabulary, and on occasion its clichés, with the ease of a familiar, and yet writing with his tongue slightly in his cheek. His style is very much his own, and in his case it is particularly true to say that the style is the man. It is an extraordinary mixture of the 'courtly' and the plebeian, almost the truculent. It is larded with proverbs, quips and puns. He will take a 'courtly' figure of speech and, with a deliberate exaggeration, topple it into absurdity. He juxtaposes the sublime and the ridiculous as though to emphasize that, while he knows the rules of the game, he is not always prepared to play it with the deadly seriousness required. One could accuse him of being too clever by half, because his knowingness can at times be irritating, but wit and brevity and elegance are commodities in too short supply for one to cavil at such trifling faults; better to be grateful for the consummate artistry with which he tells his tale.

Select Bibliography

Le Lai de l'Ombre, ed. Joseph Bédier, S.A.T.F., Paris, 1913.

Le Lai de l'Ombre, ed. John Orr, Edinburgh University Press, 1948. (It is on this edition that the translation is based, and I am particularly indebted to Professor Orr's excellent notes, as also to the help generously afforded me by Mrs D. R. Sutherland in my struggle with a notoriously difficult text.)

L'Escoufle, roman d'aventure, ed. H. Michelant and Paul Meyer, S.A.T.F., Paris, 1894.

Le Roman de la Rose ou de Guillaume de Dôle, ed. Rita Lejeune, Paris, 1936.

L'Œuvre de Jean Renart, Rita Lejeune–Dehousse, Liège–Paris, 1935. (Contains beside an important and comprehensive study of his works critical editions of *Du Plait Renart de Dammartin* and *De Renart et de Piaudoue*; also an extensive bibliography.)

The Lay of the Reflection

I have no wish to forsake my practice of telling good tales; on the contrary, I want to put my wits to some other use than idling time away. Nor do I wish to resemble those who ruin everything by their incompetence, but, since I have the talent to set forth some example deserving of esteem in word and deed, none but a churl would mock at it, particularly when my good taste displays itself in the telling of some pleasing tale devoid of ribaldry or offence. He is a fool who, knowing a good story, allows a jibe to prevent his telling it, and if some scurvy fellow should cock a snook behind his back he lets it pass, for in my opinion one could no more teach a blackguard manners than I could make this finger as long as its neighbour. It has been said before now that there's more to be gained from being born in an auspicious hour than from being one of the great. The lot of that Guillaume who dismembered the kite and burned each separate piece, as that other tale reminds us,[1] can serve to prove that I speak the truth and that fortune stands a man in better stead than wealth or friends: a friend may die, and wealth is quickly lost unless one takes good care of it; and he who entrusts it to a fool soon squanders and exhausts his store, and then his folly stands revealed in his having spent it without discretion. But if from then on he sobers down, if he quits his giddy ways and bad luck leaves him be, fortune will soon set him up again. And so I am embarking on this tale because I want to deploy my talents in composing a good poem, and bend to the eminence of the Electus.[2] It gives me great delight that his good pleasure should have chosen me for so congenial a task as putting an adventure into verse. They say it's the good helmsman who brings his ship to shore from the high seas. He who makes the port of poesy is held in higher esteem by counts and kings.[3] So listen now to what, provided I'm not hindered, I will make of the Lay of the Reflection, as I shall recount it in the following tale.

The Lay of the Reflection

There was once, as the story goes, a knight who lived in the Empire somewhere along the borders of Lorraine and Germany. I doubt whether such another could be found in all the royal domain [4] who could lay claim, as he could, to every knightly gift and virtue. In many respects he resembled the son of Lot, Gawain as we call him; but I never heard his name, nor do I know whether indeed he had one. Valour and courtesy had chosen him for their domain. All who knew him marvelled at his lavish spending, and despite his valour you would have found him neither garrulous nor conceited. He was not a rich man, but he knew how to conduct his affairs, being adept at taking money where he found it and transferring it to where it was lacking. Not a maiden or lady heard him spoken of who did not hold him in high esteem, nor did he ever make a determined set at any without being well received, for he was the most open-hearted, gracious and chivalrous of men. Within doors anyone could do whatever they wished with him, but in the pursuit of arms you would have found him the opposite of my description: daring and bold and pugnacious once his helmet was on his head. He would gallop up and down the ranks seeking an adversary for a joust. Indeed this knight I'm telling you about was come to the point where he wished there were two Mondays in every week: [5] God never made a knight so mad about jousting as he. He was not the sort to wear his summer clothes in the winter. He gave away more costly furs than many another with ten times his fortune, and always liked to have seven companions in his train, or five at the very least, and whatever he had in his hand was anyone's for the asking. He enjoyed the pleasures of falconry when opportunity allowed, for which I do not think the worse of him, and was more skilled than Tristan at chess and fencing and suchlike pastimes. For a long time he led a most agreeable life and made himself generally liked. He was a handsome man with a good figure, quick-moving and limber and light on his feet, yet great as was his physical beauty, his valour was still greater; he was, in fact, all that a knight should be.

At this propitious moment, Love, who is both man's mistress and his master, let fly at him, wishing to get the upper hand over him and take her tribute of the ample pleasure he had had of many a lady in his time: for he had neither served her nor paid her homage while he could avoid it. So, because he did not acknowledge himself her vassal, nor pay her dues, when a time and place offered, she gave him so sharp a taste of her sovereign might that that same Tristan, who, for Yseult's sake, had himself shorn as a madman,[6] did not suffer a third of the trials he endured before he finally made his peace with her. She shot her shaft into his breast right up to the feathers, implanting in his heart the radiant beauty and sweet name of a certain lady. Now every rival image had to be cast out and banished; till then his heart had flitted from one to another, loving none, but now it became most palpably plain to him that he would have to devote himself entirely to serving this beauty, who appeared to him the very pearl of all perfections. Her wit, her charm, her beauty of feature and complexion lived, as it seemed to him, day and night in his mind's eye. Thinking of her was the only pleasure he did not weary of. Love prosecuted him with such rigour that he was only too well acquainted with her power; he swore he had never seen so charming a creature in woman's form and called his eyes to witness to the truth of what he said.

'Ah, me!' he sighed, 'I have been so miserly and grudging with my affections. Now God sees fit to avenge by means of one the many who have loved me unrequited. Truly, I am well repaid for scorning those whom Love took unawares! Now Love has got me where she would have me feel the brunt of her power, for there was never a churl having his teeth drawn by the barber who was in such agony as this.'

So did he muse and reason when he was alone, and if he could, he would have done no different, for Love had put him in a crueller fix than ever a man was in.

'Alas!' he said, 'and what will come of it if I love and am not loved? I cannot say, but I do not see how I could live a single day. Neither the distractions of the road nor the pleasures of the hall are any remedy for my torment. Nothing remains but to make much of those who frequent her house, for many have won their ladies' favours by this means. If only she whom I love had made a noose for my neck with her own two arms! All night long I dream that mine are round her and that she is holding me in the closest of embraces. Waking tears me free when I'm on the point of tasting my greatest bliss. Then I feel around my bed, searching for her lovely body that burns me and sets me on fire. But, alas! "can't find doesn't get"; it has happened to me and others many a time. There is nothing else for it, I shall either have to go, or send to entreat her to show herself merciful in my regard (since there is nothing else left to me), and for God's sake to take pity on me before I die, and of her infinite kindness to preserve my life and wits. Since she would be the poorer by one liegeman if she let me die it is only right that her heart should show compassion and her eyes look gently on me. And I do believe that I would gain more by going myself than by sending to her – "a man's his own best friend", as the saying goes – and no one else would go so gladly. It has been said before that necessity is a good teacher – and privation is another. Since I have the support of a proverb it only remains to go there and tell her that my heart is her prisoner, surrendered of its own free will, and that it will never seek its freedom, come pain or hardship, until it receives the name of lover. Kindness, pity and generosity should move her to grant that much.'

He got ready to leave, taking only two companions with him. What more should I tell you? He mounted, likewise six young servants, and rode on his way communing happily with himself, intent on his reverie and on his journey. To prevent his companions guessing the reason for his expedition, he set them off on a different track from the one his thoughts were following, announcing that he was riding quite at random, and so concealed his course and purpose till they came to the look-out mound of the castle where the lady resided. This lord, who was leading the party, then exclaimed:

'See how well positioned that castle is!'

He did not say it so much because of anything special about the walls or ditches, as to see whether his luck had swung him high enough for the others to speak of the perfections of the lady he was going to see.

'You should be properly ashamed,' they said; 'it was most unseemly of you to mention the castle to us before its lovely mistress, who is said by all to be without peer in the whole kingdom for beauty and manners and breeding! So hold your peace!' they went on, 'for if she knew how you had offended it would be better for you to have been captured by the Turks and carried off to Cairo!'

The knight replied with a quick smile:

'Gently now, my lords, gently! Don't be quite so hard on me, I haven't deserved death! There's not a castle I covet excepting that. I would gladly spend five or six years in Saladin's prison provided it was assigned to me just as it is, to have and to hold, together with everything within its walls.'

'You would have the luck of a lord, then!' exclaimed his friends, who missed the double meaning in his remark, which the good knight had only made in order to hear what they would say. He asked them next whether they would go and take a look.

'What else should we do?' they asked. 'A knight ought not to pass by a beautiful lady on his travels without stopping to see her.'

'I defer to your wishes,' replied their leader, 'which are mine as well, and I recommend we go there, seeing that reason urges it.'

At that each rider turned his horse's head towards the gate with the shout:

'Knights, to the ladies!' A fitting cry for such an errand![7]

With their horses under bit and spur they cantered to the fortress, passing through a new outer bailey enclosed with palisades and ditches. The knight had thrown back his cloak off his chest, as also his rich surcoat of scarlet silk trimmed with ermine and squirrel. They all had similar garments, and were wearing white pleated shirts besides, and chaplets of periwinkles and other flowers, and red-gold spurs to boot. I do not know how they could have been more elegantly dressed for a summer's day. They never drew rein until they came to the mounting block before the hall. The squires, well trained, jumped down one to each stirrup. The steward of the house saw them dismount in the courtyard; he ran from the gallery where he was standing to inform his mistress that the man she knew so well from hearsay was coming to call on her. The lady certainly did not redden with annoyance, she was, however, greatly amazed. She had been having her hair plaited, seated on a bright red cushion, and now this beautiful creature rose to her feet. Her maidens threw a silk cloak round her shoulders, enhancing the wondrous beauty that Nature, according to report, had already endowed her with. Although she wanted to go to meet them, they, for their part, made such haste towards her that they had already entered the chamber before she had time to leave it. It appeared from her manner in greeting them that their coming pleased her: as for them, they were more than happy that she had come even so short a distance to meet them. This gracious and estimable lady was wearing a filmy white gown which trailed behind her more than a yard's length on the fine rushes.

'Welcome, my lord, to you and to your two companions,' said the lady (and a good day, too, to her this day, for she deserves as much. His companions had spoken truly when they said she was not the sort of lady one should by-pass without a visit.)

The three men stood bemused by her beauty as they returned her greeting.

Smiling, she took the knight by the hand and led him to sit down. Now that he had taken his place beside her he had a taste of his ambition. His companions knew the proprieties: they sat down, without obtruding themselves on him, on a chest banded and studded with copper beside two of her maidens. While they were sporting with them and asking them about this and that, their good lord scarcely gave them a thought, preoccupied as he was with his own affair. His noble and gracious lady however, who allied wit and sense to perfect manners, had an apt rejoinder to every subject he broached to her. His eyes were for ever on her face, drinking in her beauty; as for his heart, which was wholly hers, it had done well to trust their testimony, for they now confirmed, detail by detail, the truth of all their promises. Her face and cast of feature pleased him exceedingly.

'Fair, dear and sweetest friend,' he said, 'for whom an overwhelming love constrains me to forsake all other women and banish them from my thoughts, I have come to place all I have, my strength and the dominion that I wield, at your disposal; and may it bring me joy, for there is nothing I love as I do you, so be God grant me forgiveness at the last; and this is why I came here, wishing you to know as much, that you might be moved to magnanimity and pity, as there is truly need; for such as have a mind to offer prayers in church would do well to pray for those who are intent on nothing but being faithful lovers.'

'Ah! sir, upon my soul,' she replied, 'what are you saying? I'm quite astounded! Why this strange talk?'

'Madam,' he said, 'I am telling you the truth: of all the women on earth, you, and you alone, command me.'

Her colour quickened and glowed at hearing him say he was wholly hers. Then she said to him with a happy pertinence:

'In truth, sir, I do not believe for a moment that so handsome a man as yourself can be without a mistress; no one would credit such a thing; your valour and reputation would both decline – a man like you, with such a fine figure, hands, and arms, and all beside! Upon my honour, you would know just how to throw the dust in my eyes with clever speeches and get me to do what ought not to be done!'

With these words she succeeded in stopping him in his tracks and upset his reckoning, as I was given to understand by him who told me the story. He let himself be led on a short rein, and indeed there was nothing else he would have liked as well; if another had slighted him he would not have been at a loss to get his own back, but he was so much in her power that he dared not contradict her in anything, but merely began to sue afresh:

'Ah, madam, for pity's sake, grace! It is my love for you, and no pretence, that makes me reveal my suffering. Your words accord ill with your lovely eyes, which gave me a better welcome when I arrived just now, and a more pleasing one. And never doubt but what they acted in a seemly and fitting manner, for since the hour when they very first opened they never looked on a single man, and that's the long and the short of it, who was so honestly and unfeignedly anxious to become your vassal as I. Sweet lady, of your gracious kindness, please you to put it to the test: retain me as your knight, and, when you choose to, as your friend! For before a year and a half has passed you will have made such a man of me, both at tourney and in hall, and instilled so much of good in me that, God willing, the name of lover could never be refused me.'

'Much good may the assumption do you!' said she. 'I meant nothing by my look beyond the requirements of good manners and good sense. You read another and extravagant meaning into it, a fact which I deplore. Were I not a person of breeding and refinement I should take it very ill; but it happens often enough that when by her manner some noble lady shows a knight honour and courtesy, these suitors promptly think they have gained their own quite different ends! I found the proof of it in you: that is just how you understood it. You would have been better employed setting a net outside to catch pigeons! For if the year and a half were as long as three whole years, nothing you could perform, however hard you strove, would suffice to win you as kind a reception as I gave you earlier. A man should beware of counting his chickens before they are hatched.'

This left the knight quite at a loss as to what he should say or do, or what would become of him.

'At all events, madam,' he replied, 'I cannot be worse off than I was before. Pity and graciousness are to be found in you, of that I am sure; and no true lover ever failed to win his lady in the end. I, who have been for a long time master of my fate, have now like Tristan put to sea without a mast, to drown there. I am come to such a pass that, unless I meet with some compassion this evening, I never expect to see another dusk follow tomorrow's dawn. My heart has persecuted me so cruelly that it has lodged itself in you without a warrant.'

'I never heard such nonsense,' said she with a little smile. 'It had better rest at that, since I see it is not a joke. Just now, by St Nicholas, I thought you were making fun of me.'

'By God, not I![8] Were you but a poor, abandoned girl, fair, sweet and honourable lady, I could not bring myself to do such a thing.'

Nothing that he could say or promise furthered in the slightest his prospects of winning her favour, and he was at his wits' end. The colour rushed to his face and the fullness of his heart overflowed in tears, making pale runnels down his crimson cheeks. At this point it became clear to the lady that her heart was not misleading her; she recognized, on the contrary, that he was often in her thoughts at other times than the present. Most certainly it would have been a great relief to her to weep along with him; never could she have imagined that he would be so distressed.

'Sir,' she said then, 'it would not be right for me to love you or anyone else, for I have my husband, who is a most worthy man, and who shows me every honour and attention.'

'How fortunate, madam!' he replied. 'He must be happy indeed to do so! But if you showed yourself generous and compassionate towards me, none who celebrate love or read of it would think the worse of you for it; on the contrary, the world would gain in honour if you deigned to love me. Such charity would be tantamount to making a pilgrimage to the Holy Land.'

'Now relieve me of your presence, sir,' said she. 'This is still more offensive. My feelings absolutely forbid my agreeing to it; it is therefore a vain entreaty and I beg you to resign yourself.'

'Ah! madam,' he exclaimed, 'that is a mortal thrust, Take care you never repeat it, but do the right and courteous thing: attach me to your person with a jewel, a belt or a ring, or accept one of mine, and I swear to you, as God is my aid, that there is no service a knight can render a lady that I will not perform for you, though it should cost me my soul. Your sweet eyes and radiant countenance can retain me for a trifling gage: I am wholly at your disposal in so far as in me lies.'[9]

'Sir,' said the lady, 'I do not want the title without the dues. I am well aware that you are held in high esteem, it has long been common knowledge; and I should be playing false were I now to encourage your love without my feelings being engaged: indeed it would be contemptible. To remain above reproach, for such as can, is the highest mark of breeding.'

'To salve my hurt, madam, you must speak a different language. It would be a grave fault if you should let me die unloved, and that pretty and so candid face became my executioner. Some solution must be arrived at soon. Lady of loveliness, dispenser of every good, for God's sake look to it!'

Fair words, and so gratifying and urbane! They set her musing to the effect that she would fain admit his suit. She felt sorry for him, too; his sighs, the tears he shed, were never feigned, she said to herself: it was rather the furious assault of love that was the cause of his behaviour; and if she rejected this lover, she would never have another as noble as he. She was very surprised, though, that he had never spoken of it until today. Over against these thoughts she was nagged by reason, which conversely bade her beware of doing anything she might ultimately regret. As for the knight, hanging anxiously on the outcome of her reflections, Love, who has proved her subtlety and ingenuity over and again in these affairs, pointed his way to a gesture of perfect taste and elegance. While his noble mistress was so deep in thought he quickly took his ring from his finger and slipped it on to hers; then he capped this feat with a master-stroke by breaking her train of thought, so that she had no time to remark the ring's being on her finger. To ensure that she did not notice it:

'Your leave, madam!' he said. 'Be assured that my person and dominion are wholly at your command.'

He made a hurried exit, followed by his two companions; no one, save himself, knew the reason for his leaving in that fashion. In pensive mood and with many a sigh he went to his horse and mounted. She on whom the recovery of his happiness most depended said to herself:

'Could he really be going away? What does this mean? Such behaviour was never seen in a knight! I should have thought a whole year would have seemed far shorter than a day to him, provided he was with me, and now he has left me already! Ah me! What if I had yielded to him in word or deed! After the masquerade he put on for my benefit I'll never trust anyone again! So help me heaven, he would have been no loser if he had been believed on the strength of his sighs and his crocodile tears! It would have been the best and neatest deception ever practised, and that's a fact!'

At that point she glanced down at her hands and caught sight of the ring. All the blood drained from her body, little toe inclusive;[10] she had never been so taken aback or dumbfounded by anything. Her face, which had been flushed, grew ashen pale.

'What's this?' she exclaimed. 'God help me! Do I see his ring here? I am sufficiently in my right mind to be sure that I saw the selfsame one on his finger a short while back. Indeed I did. Just now. And why did he put it on mine? He is certainly not my lover! Yet I suspect he thinks he is. Now, by heaven, he is past master at this art; I don't know who his teacher was. Great God! how did he manage to slip it on me? Because I'm so sharp that I did not even notice his putting a ring on my finger! Now he will say that he's my lover; he will, too; of that I'm sure. And will it be true? Do I love him? No, I do not. He would be making a vain pretension. On the contrary, I shall send to him at once and bid him speak with me if he wants me to look on him as a friend, and I shall tell him to take it back. I do not think that he will offend against my wishes if he does not want me to hate him!'

With that she bade her maidens send a mounted servant in to her, and they chivvied him so much that he was already on horseback when he came before her.

'Friend,' she said, 'off with you at the gallop! Spur after the knight! Tell him, as he sets store by my friendship, not to proceed, but to return at once and speak to me on a matter that concerns him.'

'Madam,' he replied, 'I am confident I shall carry out your wishes fully.'

Thereupon he clapped in his spurs and galloped off after the knight whom Love was tormenting with thoughts of her who was sending to fetch him. In under a league the youth caught up with him and turned him back, and he, you may be sure, considered himself born under a lucky star to have been sent for. He did not ask the messenger why he had been summoned to return: the ring she had on her finger was the pretext for his recall, while her anxiety to see him was cause enough for him to change his course. The squire on the return journey struck up an acquaintance with him. Oh, God! how happy he would have been to return, had it not been for the gnawing fear that she wanted to return his ring! He said to himself that he would go for a monk to Cîteaux before he took it back, and added:

'I don't believe she would do me that offence.'

The joy of returning stifled his misgivings and soon he had covered the distance that separated him from the fortress.

The lady, who was in much distress, and fighting against her feelings, left the hall and descended the stairway step by step. Deliberately and from choice she entered the courtyard to beguile the time, and caught on her finger as she did so the glint of the ring she intended to return to the knight.

'If ever he makes difficulties about it,' she said, 'and refuses to accept it, I shan't grab him by his pretty locks on that account! Instead, if I can, I'll bring him over to this well and talk to him here. If he won't take it back without unpleasantness I shall break off the conversation at once. How? I won't be so foolish as to throw it down on the path. Where then? Somewhere where no one will see it: in the well, and that's the truth. Then there will never be any gossip that might reflect on me, no more than about a dream. It were a sorry thing for me to have lived chaste so long if this man, on the strength of a chivalrous manner and the heaving of a few sighs, would have me accept him as a lover already at this first meeting; he would have to show other deserts than those for me to yield to him.'[11]

The knight, unaware of all this, had meanwhile entered the gallery, from where he observed the lady, whose sight afforded him much pleasure, walking about the courtyard. He went down at once and ran across to her with the due urgency of a knight approaching his mistress. Neither his two companions nor any member of the household stood in his way.

'May good fortune wait this day on my lady, whose vassal I am and ever shall be!' he declared, and that was the only clip on the ear she had from him! She had heard many things already that day that had touched her to the quick.

'Sir,' she said, 'let us go over there and sit by the well to pass the time agreeably.'

He said to himself that nothing could blight his chances now, since she received him so graciously, and felt confident at that moment of winning her love and favour, thanks to his ring. But he still had a long way to travel before he could rejoice; he had not had time to seat himself beside her when he heard something to displease him.

'Sir,' she said, 'this ring of yours I hold here, for mercy's sake please tell me why you gave it to me just now?'

'Sweet lady,' he replied, 'when I leave you will have it still; believe me when I tell you – and don't think I am shamming – that its value has increased by half for having been on your finger. Provided it met with your approval, my enemies would taste my mettle this summer, if you had accepted me as a lover and I enjoyed your favour.'

'By heaven!' she said, 'there is no question of that; quite the reverse. You will never enjoy the credit and prestige afforded by my love, no matter what I see, or I'll not leave this house again, so help me God, unless it be dead. You are not on the right track at all, in fact you have gone badly astray. Here! Take your ring, please, for I want none of it. And woe betide you if you consider me your mistress on the grounds of its having been in my keeping!'

What despair and misery were now the knight's who had thought that all was won!

'If what I heard were definite, my very worth would languish. Never did I taste a joy which turned so soon to gall!'

'How so, sir?' she inquired. 'Have you received any humiliation or affront from me, who have no ties of affection or kinship with you? I am doing you no great outrage in wishing to return your ring to you. You have no option but to take it back, for I've no right to keep it since I do not want to retain you as a lover: indeed, it would be wrong of me to do so.'

'God!' he exclaimed. 'If I were to plunge a dagger into my leg it would cause me less agony than your words. To destroy and crush a man who is in one's power is a reprehensible thing. The passionate love I bear you subjects me to the cruellest of torments; and as for making me take my ring back, there's not a woman in the world who would not rue the ambition! In faith, may I never enter God's heaven if ever I take it back! No, you shall have it, and I will leave my heart along with it in your service, for your wishes will never be served so well as by my heart and ring combined.'

'Never speak of this matter again,' she replied, 'for you would forfeit my society and my trust if you insist against my wishes on making me angry with you. It behoves you to take it back.'

'It does not.'

'It does, and there's no more to say; else you will be exceeding the rights of a lord and master, if you carry your importunity so far as to force your ring on me, despite myself. Here, take it!'

'I never wish to lay finger on it again.'

'You shall, though.'

'Indeed I shall not.'

'Do you want to thrust it on me by force?'

'No, indeed, dear friend; I am well aware that I have not that authority, and, as God is my help, I regret it! It is my belief that no hurt or sorrow could ever overtake me if you gave me a ray of hope to encourage me.'

'You might as well knock your head against this stone surround as hope to succeed in that; so I advise you to take it back.'

'It seems to me you are teaching me to repeat myself.[12] I would let my neck be rubbed bare by the hangman's rope before I took it back.[13] I don't know how I could make you a long speech on the subject, for there is no question of my taking it back.'

'Sir,' she said, 'it is clear to me now that your behaviour stems from pure obstinacy, since nothing I can say can induce you to accept it. Now I will conjure you by the great faith you owe me, and entreat you, as you value your love for me, to take your ring again.'

Now, by the love of God, there were no two ways about it: either he must take it back or she would hold him for a knave or a vain prater.

'God!' he thought, 'which horn of this dilemma will prove the least damaging to me? It's plain enough that if I leave her the ring she will say I do not love her. To squeeze the crust so hard as to force out the crumb is to overdo the squeezing. This oath has got me in such a corner that it is not in my interest to leave her the ring. On the contrary, I think it would be more to my profit and honour to take it back, if I do not want to show grave disrespect towards my revered lady who has conjured me by my love and the great faith I owe her. Even when it is on my finger it will still be hers. If I do what she asks of me nothing but honour can accrue to me. He is no true lover who does not do his mistress' bidding to the limit, and to leave what can be done undone is not to love. I must fit my conduct entirely to her will and pleasure, for nothing must be but as she wishes it.'

He said then, using a formal address:

'Madam, I will take it on this condition: that, having done your pleasure, I please myself what I do with it after, for all it has been on this finger which is so lovely in my eyes.'

'And I then return your ring on that understanding.'

The brains of this valiant knight had not mouldered away or run to seed. His heart on fire with love, he took the ring with deliberation and looked at it tenderly, and as he took possession of it he said:

'My grateful thanks: being on your pretty finger has kept the gold from tarnishing!'

The lady smiled at this, thinking he would put it back on his own; but instead he did something much more astute which was to bring him his fill of joy. Resting his elbows on the wall of the well, which was only a fathom and a half deep, he did not miss noticing in the clear, limpid water the reflection of the lady whom he adored above all things on earth.

'Be assured once and for all,' he said, 'that I will not take it home: it shall go to my sweet mistress, the thing I love next best to you.'

'Heavens!' she cried, 'there are only us two here; where can you have found her so quickly?'

'Before God, you shall look this very minute on the noble and excellent lady who is to have it.'

'Where is she then?'

'Upon my soul, see, there she is! Your lovely reflection waiting there for it.'

He took the ring and held it out to her:

'Here!' he said, 'my own sweet love! Since my lady will none of it, you will surely take it without our coming to blows.'

The water rippled slightly as the ring fell in; and, as the reflection shivered and broke up, he exclaimed:

'See, madam! Now she's taken it. My standing is much enhanced by the fact of its being accepted by a counterpart of you. If only there were a door or gate below, that she might come up here so that I could thank her for the honour she has done me!'

Great God! What a happy thing for him to find his way to making so delicate a gesture! No action of his had ever charmed the lady so much. With quickened vivacity, and all aglow, she turned her eyes to his. A rich reward is theirs who have the wit to be elegant at need.

'To think how far I was from loving this man a few moments ago and how close to my heart he is now! Never in any age since Adam bit into the apple has a man lit on so exquisite a gesture; I cannot imagine how he thought it up. If for love of me he can throw his ring to my reflection in the well I cannot nor ought not to refuse him my favours any longer. Why I keep him waiting I cannot think, for never was love so well or prettily won with a ring, nor did ever a man so richly deserve to have a mistress.'

You may be sure she did not offend him when she said:

'Most fair, sweet friend, your heart and mine have been made as one by these gracious words and pleasing ways, and by the gift you made to my shadow in my honour. Now put my ring on your finger. Here, I give it to you as a token of my love. I dare say you will not like it less than your own, even if it is poorer.'

'The lordship of the Empire would not make me as happy,' he replied.

They took as much pleasure as they could there by the well, and that was no mean measure. They regaled each other with kisses whose sweetness pierced them both to the heart, while their eyes did not disdain their share, to say the least of it. As for such play as lovers' hands contrive, both she and he were free to show their skill, except for what the occasion disallowed, and that in time would be well remedied.

There is no need now for Jehan Renart to give any further thought to their concerns; if he has something else to do he can turn his mind to that. For since Love and their mother wit have combined to unite their hearts, it's my opinion that they will manage quite well on their own as regards the sport remaining. So let's have silence on the subject from now on! Here ends the Lay of the Reflection: re-count it now, you tellers![14]

THE DAPPLE-GREY PALFREY

Introduction

O F the five tales collected here this is perhaps the one that requires the least comment, but what it lacks in profundity or incidental interest is happily outweighed by the merits of the story itself. It is a simple and pleasing tale of a poor but otherwise admirable knight who aspires to the hand of a rich lord's daughter. His love is reciprocated, but the father, needless to say, views the match with a more than jaundiced eye. The lovers light on a crafty scheme for overcoming his opposition to their marriage, but the plan, as even the best-laid will, backfires in an unexpected way. Treachery however reaps its own reward, and in the end the tables are turned again, this time to the lovers' advantage, and it is very much a case of he laughs best who laughs last.

The earliest known version of the story is to be found in an appendix to the fables of Phaedrus, and scholars hold it to be from his pen. There is also a fifteenth-century prose version, entitled *De Erard de Voysines, qui espousa Philomena*, which adheres more closely to the Latin original. In between, the tale in one form or another must have featured in many an entertainer's repertory, refashioned each time to suit the audience or the teller's fancy. The author of the *Vair Palefroi* gives himself as one Huon le Roi. He is probably to be identified with a certain Huon le Roi de Cambrai who composed a number of pious works in the middle and later years of the thirteenth century, the most distinguished of which is the *Regrés Nostre Dame*. There are also three other *fabliaux*, passing indifferent, which might conceivably be by the same hand, though this is far from proven.* There is nothing here that betokens a great poet, but he was obviously a professional and must have enjoyed the regard of his contemporaries to have been, as his title would suggest, the president of his local guild.

Like Jean Renart, he had an excellent opinion of himself and his

---

* Cf. J. Bédier, *Les Fabliaux*, Paris, 1925, pp. 482–3 and *Huon le Roi: le Vair Palefroi*, ed. Långfors, Introduction.

talents, but the kindest adjective that can be applied to his style in *The Dapple-grey Palfrey* is pedestrian. His verse is competent, if somewhat cliché-ridden, but he has all the faults of the medieval poet intent on displaying his modicum of learning: he is long-winded, repetitive and banal. And here I must confess to having covered up for him to a certain extent and used what seems to me allowable translator's licence, varying the restricted vocabulary and taking minor liberties with the syntax in order to make it reasonably flowing. In fairness to the reader, though, who might wish to compare tale with tale, it must be stated that the standard of writing in this story falls well below that of the others, at least in those passages which treat of the lovers' concerns.

If parts of the work leave much to be desired stylistically the whole has many undeniable qualities. Firstly it is an excellent story, full of twists and turns and surprises. It is narrated with verve, particularly in the latter stages where the events leading up to the discomfiture of the 'ancients' are detailed with malicious enjoyment. The characterization is minimal, as is only to be expected in a story where the plot is all-important, but the author submits the social scene to a cool, if amused, appraisal. He is less concerned with the refinements of manners and behaviour than with the harsher realities underlying them. The landscape he depicts for us is less idealized than some; one expects it to rain here, and mud to clog the axle-trees, and armour to rust up; and love is all very fine, but land-rents weigh more heavily in the scales. He is an adept at sketching a scene: the two old men swapping tales over their mulled wine; the fuddled night-watchman blinking at the moon-light and mumbling to himself; the cavalcade of doddering knights jogging three parts asleep through the interminable forest. These and many more stick in the mind, imprinted there by the author's gift for describing in a few strokes of the pen human foibles observed with a dispassionate but not unsympathetic eye.

The work was classed by its first editors as a *fabliau* and accepted as such by Bédier. It is one of some half dozen love stories which, by their theme and treatment, rise above the general level of scur-rility which characterizes the genre. To class it as a *fabliau* though is surely right. The *fabliaux* have been defined as '*contes à rire*' and this, despite some highflown sentiments and lovers' sighs, is basically what it is. It is the story of a mean trick paid back, if not in kind, at any rate with interest. There is no exploration of character; indeed there is little character to explore. But, without any aspirations to literary significance, it has gaiety and charm, and as entertainment surely deserves an honourable mention.

EDITIONS

Recueil Général des Fabliaux, A. de Montaiglon, 1872, Vol. I.

Huon le Roi: Le Vair Palefroi, ed. Artur Långfors, Classiques Français du Moyen Age, Paris, 1912.

Li Regrés Nostre Dame, par Huon le Roi de Cambrai, Paris, 1907.

La Vie de Saint Quentin, par Huon le Roi de Cambrai, Långfors and Söderhjelm, Helsingfors, 1909.

Œuvres (Li Abécés par Ekivoche, Li Ave Maria en Roumans, La Descrissions des Relegions), Huon le Roi de Cambrai, ed. Långfors, Paris, 1913.

The Dapple-grey Palfrey

IT is as a reminder and portrayal of the blessings, tenderness and generosity of spirit which can be elicited from womankind that this history has been recorded, for it behoves one to recall to mind the good that's to discover there. Indeed it is a matter of the keenest sorrow and regret to me that women do not meet on every hand with the praise and appreciation they deserve. Ah, God! had they but whole and undivided hearts, tempered and true, the wide world could not boast so great a treasure. How regrettable and sad it is that they do not keep a better watch over themselves; it takes but little to change them, they are quick to face about and bend to the wind. In truth, their hearts resemble weathercocks, for it is no unusual thing to see their feelings change in less time than it takes a thunderstorm to gather. Since I have undertaken this work at a particular request, there is no inconstant, fickle knave, venting his envious spleen on those of finer and more noble metal, that shall discourage me from seeing it through to the end, a spur alike to my pleasure and my fame. So, in this lay of the 'Dapple-grey Palfrey' you will hear a matter rationally unfolded according to the lights of Huon le Roi, he having acquired an understanding of reason and wishing, too, to set out some of his verses, since, in his view, he is putting them to excellent account.

Now the story relates that in the county of Champagne there lived a most valorous and courtly knight, whose heart was high but whose funds were low, as you will have occasion to discover. It is meet that I should describe his merits and the valour that animated him, since in many and sundry quarters he was held in high regard as a man of judgement, honour and distinction, stouthearted in the extreme. Had he been as loaded with wealth as he was fired with excellence (saving he grew the worse for having it), he would have been without peer or fellow; and, since the deeds of gallant men should be recounted in full to serve as good and gratifying examples, I am setting out to chronicle his story.

Wherever he went this knight was praised by one and all; his reputation was so widely known that those who had not met him loved him by repute for being the fountain-head of so much good. At tournaments, when his head was iron-clad, he had no time for dallying with the ladies outside the barricades; there where the press was thickest he would hurl himself full tilt: no novice he, when he was armed and mounted. There was never a day in the depths of winter when he did not sport a gay gown, which could be seen to reflect his sunny disposition. His good cheer was the more admirable in that his holding was of little value: his lands did not bring him in above two hundred pounds a year, and so it was that he travelled far and wide in search of renown. The woodlands and countryside of Champagne were wilder then than they are today.

The knight was much taken up this time with an honest and noble passion for a high-born maiden, the daughter of a worthy prince, a man of might and substance; far from being in want, he had an abundance of goods and chattels, and his coffers were well filled. His lands were worth at least a thousand pounds a year to him, and he had many requests for the hand of his charming daughter whose great beauty was a lure to all and sundry. This prince was a widower in the decline of life who had no other children; his castle stood amid deep woods, encircled by a wide expanse of forest. The other knight in my story aspired to the hand of this knight's daughter, but her father opposed his suit, neither wanting him to love her nor her to be gossiped about on his account. The young knight went by the name of Sir William, and he too lived in the forest where the rich old lord dwelled, well entrenched in his vast lands and great possessions. The manors were two leagues apart, but there was no keeping love within their confines, for the two young people did not dissipate their mental energies on extraneous matters. When the knight wished to meet with his beloved, because of idle talk about him and her he took a path he had made through the dense sweep of the forest, and which was not frequented by a living soul but him. Many a time he followed its sequestered course to see the maiden, riding along on his palfrey without noise or clatter. But the difficulties were great:

he could not speak to her at close quarters as he longed to do, for the courtyard was stoutly fenced and walled. The maiden dared not pass the gate, but she had such solace as was afforded her by speaking to him frequently through the planking of a palisade. A deep ditch on the outside and a dense bank of thorn bushes prevented their drawing close. The castle stood on a rock; it was strongly fortified and had a drawbridge at the entrance. As for the old knight, who had guile enough for any contingency and whose life was nearly spent, he rarely left the house, being past riding, but stayed at home in peace. He had his daughter closely watched, and she often sat with him to entertain him, which was not to her taste, for she was deprived of the pleasure on which her heart was set. The good knight meanwhile, who was a man of sense, did not let the grass grow under his feet; when he saw there was no alternative he gave up asking for permission to see her, but regularly visited her abode, although he could not cross the threshold. He did not see the lovely prisoner at nearly such close range as his heart desired, and for all his frequent visits he had little to feast his eyes on, for there was no place that she could reach which afforded him a full view of her face, and both the lovers declared that their hearts were breaking.

The knight, who could not but adore a maiden whose perfections set her far above all others, had, so the story affirms, a magnificent palfrey of the most brilliant dapple grey. It would be impossible to pick out any flower that could compare with it for beauty of form or hue, nor was there a kingdom at that time which could boast so fine a creature or so quiet and comfortable a ride. The knight thought the world of it and, I tell you truly, would not have parted with it for a fortune. Over a long period it was seen in his possession by the people of the locality. He would often set off on this palfrey to woo the maiden, riding through the lovely deeps of the forest where he had trodden the track unknown to any save himself and his horse. He was careful to set up no clatter when he went to visit his beloved: he had to be on his guard lest he attracted her father's notice, for his journey would then have had a bitter ending. And this was the life they led, week in, week out, each yearning for the other and both unable to satisfy their craving with kisses or embraces. I assure you that if their lips had met the contact would have been infinitely sweet to both. Indeed this fire which they had no means of quenching burned with fever heat: for, had they been able to fondle and embrace and cling to one another, and tenderly clasp each other in their arms, as was their dream and wish and keen desire, they would have been proof against all human malice and their joy had been complete. But they were sorely deprived in being unable to touch one another and slake their ardour. In fact, these lovers had little enough delight, save that of speaking, and hearing the other's voice; they had but niggardly glimpses of each other on account of the harsh proscription laid on them. She went in dread of her father, for had he known of their understanding he would have married her the sooner, while the knight was loth to do anything which might lead to the dissevering of their love, for he stood in great awe of the ancient who was enormously powerful, and did not wish to provoke an open clash. Day after day the knight racked his brains and brooded on the life he was leading, which haunted him continually. At last he determined that, whether it turned to joy or anguish, he would go and speak to the old man and ask him for his daughter's hand whatever might befall, for he did not know what would become of him if he went on as he was doing: so strait was the road to his goal that every day of the week saw him thwarted of his desire.

One day he equipped himself for the road and made a bee-line for the place where the old man and his daughter lived, intending to beard the former. He was courteously received, being well known both to the ancient and his household. Thereupon this affable and worthy knight who, lacking no virtue, was perforce eloquent as well, said to the elder:

'Sir, I am here by your good grace: please you now to listen to my matter. I have come to your house to ask a boon of you, which I pray God may suffer you to grant me.'

The ancient gave him a long look and then said to him:

'Well then? Tell me what it is. By my faith, I will help you if I can do so without prejudice to my honour.'

'Indeed, sir, I am well enough acquainted with your situation to know that you can; God grant now that you see your way to doing so.'

'I will if it suits me; and if it is something that is not to my liking I shall know how to put a stop to it. I'm not the man to flatter you with talk of giving or promising if I've no intention of according it.'

'Sir,' said the knight, 'I will tell you the boon I would ask of you: you are not unacquainted with my life and situation; you knew my father well, you know my castle and my house, and the propriety of my conduct at all times can be no secret to you. In recompense of my deserts, sir, I ask the hand of your daughter, if it please you. God grant you to be not so indisposed by my temerity in asking you this favour that you refuse it me. I would wish you to know, too, that I was never at any time on close terms with her; I should have been a proud fellow indeed if I had talked with her and seen for myself the perfections for which she is so renowned and which have won her the love of all the people hereabouts. From what her familiars tell me, she hasn't her equal here below; but living so confined a life her intimates are few. I have been most presumptuous in venturing to ask you for her hand, and, if my suit meets with such approval that you deign to grant me this boon as a guerdon of my service, I shall be filled with pride and joy. Now I have put my petition to you: let me know your pleasure in the matter.'

The old man, without pause for thought or seeking any advice in the case, gave him his answer:

'I understand what you have said to me well enough. There is no great calumny entailed: my daughter is beautiful, young and virtuous, and comes of a great lineage, and I am a powerful vassal, sprung from noble stock, with lands that bring in a thousand pounds a year; I am not so drunk as to give my daughter to a knight who lives off his winnings at tournaments, seeing she is the only child I have; she has not forfeited my love, and all I have will be hers when I am gone. I want to marry her well. I do not know of a prince in this realm, no, not from here to Lorraine, of such wisdom, valour and virtue as would make her less than a worthy match for him. One such asked me for her hand the other day, not a month since, a man with land-rents of five hundred pounds which would be ceded to me if I cared to busy myself about it. But my daughter can afford to wait, for I am so laden with this world's goods that she runs no risk of losing her standing or seeing her marriage price diminish: she can easily have the greatest baron in all the country between here and the borders of Germany, counts and kings apart.'

This speech was a bitter blow to the knight's pride. Tarrying not a moment longer he took his leave and rode away. He was at a loss, though, as to what to do, still groaning as he was beneath the rigours of Love's tyranny.

The maiden learned of her father's refusal and what he had said, and was much distressed at heart. She was not flighty in her affections, quite the contrary; the constancy of her feelings towards her lover passes description. Before he made his way home, in anger and harsh grief, the two of them talked together outside and spoke what was in their minds. The knight related to her her father's reply and the breach between them.

'Noble and honourable maid,' he said, 'what shall I do? I have a mind to leave the country and rove the land as a masterless man, for my desire is come to naught. I cannot hope to win you now, and what will become of me I do not know. Alas that I ever had any commerce with the riches which set your father so high in his own regard! I should have loved you better with less fortune, for your father would have appreciated what I have, had he himself not had such great possessions.'

'Indeed,' she replied, 'if I had my way, I would wish to have much less than is my lot. Sir, if only my father would take your deserts into account, upon my faith I should not have to worry about your not winning my hand and his approval; if he weighed your fortune against your great prowess, the bargain must be to his liking; but his head is master of his heart, he does not want what I want nor suffer where I smart. If he fell in with my way of thinking the matter would be settled at once, but a heart that is in the grip of age has no thought for youth and its desires. The old and the young, it seems to me, have very different ambitions. However, if you do as I would have you, you cannot fail to win me.'

'Upon my faith, sweet maid, that will I, without fail,' replied the knight. 'Just tell me what you want.'

'I have been thinking,' said she, 'of something which has been in my mind for a long time. You know, of course, that you have an uncle who is very rich; he holds sway over a vast domain, and in wealth and might he is my father's equal. He has neither child, wife, nor brother, nor any closer kin than you, and it is known for a fact that on his death it will all be yours. His treasure and rents are worth more than sixty gold marks. Go over now to see him without a moment's delay. He is old and failing as you know; explain to him that you have mooted an understanding with my father that will never be clinched unless he agrees to mediate. But if he would promise you land enough to bring you three hundred pounds in rent, and were to come in person to make this application to my father who holds him in affection (for each declares the other to be an excellent man, and your uncle esteems my father for his judgement – they are old men both, and full of years, and each swears by the other), if, as I say, your uncle proved so kindly disposed to you that you could prevail on him to promise you such an advance on his estate and to say to my father besides: "My nephew will receive a portion of my domain with a rentable value of three hundred pounds against your daughter's hand: it will be a good match," then I am sure he would consent to it, if your uncle were to put it to him like that. And having married me, you would then hand back to your uncle the lands he had promised you. I am so wholly committed to your love that I should be only too happy with the bargain.'

'Believe me, fair maid,' replied the knight, 'I never wanted anything as much. I will put it to my uncle right away.'

He took his leave and rode off the way he had come, plunged in the black and gloomy thoughts begotten by the refusal he had met with. As he rode through the forest astride his dapple-grey palfrey the dismay he felt was none the less much lightened by the prudent and honest counsel that the maiden had given him. He rode without let or hindrance straight to Medet where his uncle lived. On his arrival he poured out his tale of woe and despondency. The two of them retired to a chamber over the main door and there he confided to his uncle how matters stood between himself, the maiden and her father.

'Uncle,' he said, 'if you would be so good as to put in a word for me and promise me lands worth three hundred pounds a year, I will covenant and pledge you here and now, with my hand in yours, that as soon as I have married the girl who has just been refused me, you will have your lands back unconditionally and without a quarrel, in requital of your good offices. Now, pray you, do what I ask of you.'

'Gladly, nephew,' said the uncle, 'for it gives me great pleasure and satisfaction. Upon my soul, you shall make the best match in all the land, and I am confident of bringing it about.'

'Then, uncle, expedite my business, and arrange things so that it only remains for me to wed her, for I do not want to waste any more of my life. Meanwhile I shall go to the tournament, accoutred with all magnificence; it is to be held at Gallardon, and may God grant me as a guerdon to acquit myself so well that it redound to my profit in this affair of mine: and do you put your mind to furthering my business so that I may marry on my return.'

'Most willingly, dear nephew; I am delighted at the news, for she is a girl of high and noble birth.'

With that Sir William tarried no longer but hastened on his way, in the seventh heaven of happiness at hearing his uncle say that he should most certainly have for wife the girl whom he desired: there was no bliss to be preferred to that. All alight with joy, he set off for the tournament in the manner of one whose wont it was.

Next morning at daybreak his uncle mounted and, together with six companions, arrived before prime at the place where the aged father of this paragon of beauty had his lordly mansion. He was received with much ceremony: the old man had a great affection for him, for he was his fellow in years and a rich and powerful neighbour to boot. He was gratified and elated that so great a baron should have come to visit him, and did not neglect to bid him a courteous welcome. A sumptuous meal was prepared, for the ancient was every inch a nobleman and knew how to pay honour where it was due. When the tables had been carried out, then was the time for swapping tales of past encounters with sword and shield and lance, and all their bygone glories were relived in many a stirring yarn. At length, loth to forget the purpose of his visit, the good knight's uncle disclosed what was on his mind and said straight out to his aged friend:

'What's the good of my yarning away? As God is my help you will soon find out how much I love you: I have come to you to see about a certain request which I would make of you: I pray God so to dispose you that my suit may meet with the approval that will enable me to achieve my ends.'

'Upon my soul,' replied the ancient, 'I hold you in such high esteem that nothing you could ask of me would be refused you, though it were greatly to my detriment: on the contrary any boon you solicit will be granted.'

'Sir, allow me to render you the tribute of my gratitude,' said the other old man, anxious to put his request without more delay: 'I have come to ask you, good sir, for the hand of your most virtuous daughter: I wish to take her in marriage, and before I wed her she shall be dowered out of my fortune, for I am a man of wealth and substance. You are well aware that I have no natural heirs, to my regret; I will deal honourably by her, for I have a great regard for you. After I marry your daughter I shall never seek to part our persons or our interests; on the contrary, our lands shall be united and we will hold in common what God has given us.'

The old man, with his native shrewdness, was delighted with the offer and said in reply:

'Sir, without question I will give her to you gladly, for you are a worthy man and true. I am happy that you have asked me for her hand, I should not be as joyful were I given the best castle in Friesland. In the matter of her marriage, sir, I favoured no one like yourself, for I have always found you a man of sterling worth and good counsel in every matter in which I have had dealings with you.'

Thereupon the girl, who thought to wed another, was affianced and pledged to the man she did not want.

When she learned the truth of the matter she was heart-broken and dismayed, and swore repeatedly by the Virgin Mary that he should never have her to wife. Shedding tears of bitter grief, time and again she cried out in her misery:

'Alas, unhappy wretch that I am, this is the end of me! What a shameful trick that old man played! Death would be too good for him! How vilely he has deceived his nephew, such a good and noble knight and rich in every virtue. Now, thanks to his wealth and might, I am already bestowed on that old greybeard. May God give him his just deserts! He has meddled in pure madness, for I shall never know a day's happiness again and he will have got himself a mortal enemy the day he marries me. What? shall I live to see that day? Heaven forbid! God grant my sojourn be too short to see it! Meanwhile there's grief and misery for me. Never did I hear of such vile treachery! If I were not kept so close confined I should put a stop to this business, but I can do not a thing about it, nor get away from this manor. As it is I shall have to stay and submit to what my father wants – but it is too bitter to bear! Ah God! what will become of me, and when will he who has been so shamefully betrayed be able to get back? If he but knew how his uncle had dealt with him and that I was lost to him for ever – and were that to be I know I should go down to a joyless grave – if he but knew it, upon my soul, I am confident he would put matters straight, and then my troubles would be at an end. God! how heavy my heart is! I would sooner die than live. What treachery and envy! How did that old man dare so much as think of it? No one can protect me from him, either, for cupidity, my father's cherished weakness, is too keen a goad. Fie upon old age and riches! No one now will ever be able to have a wife who is well-born and richly dowered unless his coffers are filled to overflowing. Well may I hate the wealth that separates me from the man I claim as mine, and who is certain in his mind that I'll be his; but it's my belief that I have lost him now.'

The maiden, at this juncture, was thus giving full rein to her grief, for she was, I would have you know, in a very sorry plight, what with her heart being caught so fast in the toils of love that she was hard put to it to conceal her thoughts from those around her, and filled no less with hatred for the man on whom her father had bestowed her. She considered herself ill-portioned in that he was a very old man, far gone in years, with a heavily wrinkled face and rheumy, malevolent eyes. In all the length and breadth of the land that lies between Châlons and Beauvais there was not an older knight than he, nor was there a wealthier this side of Sens, or so it was said; but in the country round he was thought devious and cruel. As for the maiden, the flame of beauty and virtue burned so high in her that there wasn't a woman in the realm of France with such perfection of looks and breeding and manners. But the apportionment was disparate indeed: light on the one hand, darkness on the other; no shadow on the light, no gleam of light in the darkness. The girl, who was racked and spurred by love, would have given a lot to be in a different posture. As for him to whom she was betrothed and who took great delight in her, he had arranged his business satisfactorily and fixed his wedding day, his mind unclouded by suspicion. He little knew her grief, or the desperate struggle provoked by love's tight hold on her heart which you have heard me describe.

I must on no account sell you short as regards the weddingtide. The wise old worthies made magnificent preparations. Before the third day came round, the father made sure of inviting all the greybeards whose sense and judgement he respected, and such as were born and bred in the region, to attend the sumptuous marriage of his daughter, whose affections were bestowed elsewhere. She had set her heart and ambitions on the excellent and illustrious knight, but realized now that she was hopelessly tricked and trapped. The two old knights had mustered a great company; all the venerable grandsires round about knew of the wedding, and most of them had come, so that there were some thirty or more assembled. There was not one who did not hold some land or benefice of the old man, and they were come now under his roof. After some parleying it was settled that the maiden should be married at daybreak, and orders were given for her to be attired by her maids-in-waiting who, on considering the day and hour appointed, were most put out and pulled long faces at the news. The father asked those to whom the instructions had been given if his daughter was ready, and if she was at all nervous, and whether anything was lacking that she ought to have.

'Nothing, good sir, that we know of,' answered one of her maidens, 'provided we have enough palfreys and saddles to take us all to the church, for I expect there will be a great crowd of kinswomen and cousins who live in the vicinity.'

'We are not unduly worried about palfreys,' he replied, 'I think we shall have enough. There is not a baron in the neighbourhood who has not been asked to send one.'

The squire to whom this mission had been entrusted lost no time in going to the house of that knight who was a very repository of valour and a shining light of prowess. The sage and noble William little thought that the marriage negotiations had reached such a stage, but the tug of love at his heartstrings had brought him hurrying home. He could think of nothing but the matter that obsessed him: love blossomed in his heart. He had returned from the tournament in a far from dismal mood, for he fully expected to wed the maiden who had so recently been refused him as soon as God willed and the occasion offered. Each day he waited on the coming of glad tidings, expecting his uncle to send him word to go and wed his wife. He sang as he went about the house, and had a minstrel play a new air on his viol; having won outright the prize of the tournament he was in the best and blithest of spirits. His glance was for ever straying towards the gate to see whether anyone was bringing him news, and he wondered constantly when the hour of his summons would come; from time to time, constrained by Love, he left his singing to brood on his heart's desire.

But now of a sudden a squire came riding into the courtyard. When Sir William caught sight of him his heart leaped in his breast, a-flutter with joy.

'God save you, sir,' said the messenger. 'I have been sent here on an errand by the ancient who is, as you know, your friend of long standing. You have a priceless palfrey, there's not a horse in the world with smoother paces; my lord sends you a pressing request to lend it him for friendship's sake, so that he may have it by tonight.'

'For what purpose, friend?'

'Sir, to take his daughter, our lovely and charming young mistress, to the church.'

'And wherefore will she be going?'

'Why, good sir, to wed your uncle, to whom she has been given. Tomorrow at daybreak my mistress is to be taken up to the lonely chapel at the far end of the forest. Make haste, sir, I stay too long; lend your uncle and my lord your palfrey – the best there is in the kingdom, that I know: it's been put to the proof time and again.'

Sir William, on hearing this, exclaimed:

'God! is it true I've been betrayed by my uncle in whom I put my trust and whom I entreated so civilly to help me in my enterprise? May the Almighty never forgive him his treachery and crime! I can scarcely credit his doing such a thing; I don't believe you are telling the truth.'

'You will be able to verify it tomorrow before the hour of prime is rung; there's already a great gathering of the old knights of the country.'

'Alas!' cried the other, 'how vilely I have been betrayed and tricked!'

He was on the point of collapsing in a faint from shock and grief and was only saved by his fear of incurring the poor opinion of his household; he was so stricken and incensed that he did not know what to do or say. He abandoned himself to his grief, and while he was in this state of agitation the messenger continued to press his suit:

'Sir, have your good palfrey saddled quickly, and seeing it is so smooth a ride it can carry my mistress up to the church.'

The knight, meanwhile, who was quietly taking his time, for he intended savouring his grief as he chewed over the bitterness of the decision he must take, namely if he would send his grey palfrey to the man he had most cause to hate, said of a sudden to himself:

'Yes, she who is so estimable, and who is now lost to me for good, is an innocent victim, to my great regret. I shall place my palfrey at her service to make her some requital for all that I have found in her of courtesy and honour, for she's possessed of every virtue, as I have verified; and now the fount is dry as far as I'm concerned, of that I can be sure. Yet there's no sense in what I have just said; on the contrary, I am a dastard and a raving fool to think of sending my palfrey to promote the joy and glee of the man who

98

has stabbed me in the back. Has he not cheated me of the girl I thought to have? No man is called upon to love the person who hatches treachery against him. He is a brazen fellow to ask me for my palfrey or anything else I have. Shall I send it to him, then? Indeed I won't. Has he not deprived me of the sweetness and beauty and wondrous grace of manner for which my beloved is prized? The long service which I vowed her is all vain now; I should by deserts have enjoyed the greater part of that sublime and sovereign good, but there's little joy it will afford me now. How can I send anything which might contribute to his happiness to the man who has utterly destroyed mine? None the less, whatever it costs me to send my palfrey for her in whom all good resides to ride upon, I know that when she sees it she will be put in mind of me. I have loved her in good faith, and do love her and always shall, but I pay a cruel price for doing so. Still will I love her, for myself alone, not knowing whether the old familiarity for which my heart aches so will still be dear to hers. I am sure he cannot be to her liking: Cain himself, the brother of Abel, did not commit a fouler crime. My heart is wrung with grief for her whose solace I'm denied.'

Venting his anguish in this fashion he had the palfrey saddled and the squire called over; and so he despatched his dapple-grey palfrey to his rival, and the messenger set off at once.

Sir William knew no respite from his misery; sick with grief and anger he shut himself in his room and announced to all his servants that if there were any so bold as to make a show of mirth he would have him hanged or done away with. He himself had lost all taste for merriment and wished only to lead a quiet, sequestered life, for nothing could rid him of the grief that weighed so heavily on his heart. Meanwhile the squire, to whom he had entrusted his palfrey, led it away and had soon got back to the castle where his lord, in festive mood, was making merry. The night was calm and still. The house was thronged with knighthood's veteran ranks. After a copious meal the ancient gave orders to the watch and informed the entire household that they were all to be awake and ready, and no lagging, and have the horses and palfreys harnessed and saddled up without rumpus or upheaval a good half hour before dawn; and with that they went to bed to get some sleep. There was one whose sighs and trembling fears, induced by Love, made sleep but a vain hope; she never shut her eyes that night; while the others slept she waked and watched. Her heart knew no repose, intent as it was on its grieving, and had she found an opportunity she would not have waited for the knights to stir or day to break, but would have slipped off quickly on her own.

Shortly after midnight the moon rose, flooding the sky and all the ambient scene with light, and when the watchman saw, through his drink-bleared eyes, how bright it was all round him, he thought that day had dawned.

'The knights and barons should have been up a while ago,' he said to himself, and thereupon announced the dawn with clarion calls and shouts.

'Arise, my lords, the dawn is breaking!' he cried, all fuddled with the wine he had drunk that evening. The household, who had rested little and slept less, stumbled dazedly to their feet; the squires made haste to saddle up, thinking dawn would soon be upon them: but before the peep of day they would have time to cover five good leagues at an easy pace. The palfreys were saddled, and all the aged knights who were to accompany the maid to her marriage service in the old chapel at the farthest end of the deep and desolate forest had mounted, and the girl was entrusted to the sagest of them all. The saddle was set on the dapple-grey palfrey, and when it was led up the maiden's grief broke out more violently than before. The old men in their wisdom were quite oblivious of what was going on in her mind, but imagined that she was weeping at leaving her father's house for a strange hearth: the cause of her tears and unbridled grief escaped them utterly. It was with great difficulty that she was mounted at all.

They all set out in a group and headed, as I remember, straight for the forest; they found the path too narrow to permit their riding two abreast and those who formed the maiden's escort fell to the rear while the rest went on ahead. The knight who rode on her right hand, seeing the way so strait, placed her in front while he fell in behind her, as the narrowness of the track commanded.

The road was interminably long and they were tired and jaded from lack of sleep, in fact they were just about worn out, and their age made the ride more gruelling still, that, and there being a good while yet to go before the dawn, which added to their heaviness. Over hill and dale they rode, nodding on their horses' necks. The most venerable had been chosen to lead the maiden, but he, that night, had had but little rest in his bed, and he had such an overwhelming desire to sleep that it betrayed him into forgetting everything beside. The maiden was horsewoman enough to sustain no hurt save that which love and sorrow caused her. As she rode down this narrow path I have described the whole great company of knights and barons was dozing off. Most of them were slumped in the saddle; a few were awake, their thoughts anywhere but on the business of escorting the maiden. On and on they jogged on their weary way through the deep forest, with the maiden, in her anguish, wishing she were in London or in Winchester.

The dapple-grey palfrey was well acquainted with this narrow, disused track, having plodded along it on many occasions. They picked their way down a steep incline where the forest was so dense that the moonlight hardly penetrated it: the shade of the close woodland was particularly thick down in the deep-sunk valley bottom. The horses' hoofs made a great clatter. The bulk of the concourse was in front, some of the barons half asleep, the others awake and talking as they rode along. Now as I understand it, the grey palfrey, which the maiden was riding in the wake of the main body, was not familiar with the farther reaches of the track that the rest of the party was now entering on, but spied a little path to the right which led straight towards Sir William's habitation. At the sight of this path, which it had often followed, it left the main track and the bevy of horses without a moment's hesitation. The knight who was detailed to escort the maiden had fallen so deeply asleep that from time to time his palfrey stopped by the way, and the maiden was left with none to convoy her but God. She loosed the reins and gave the palfrey its head, and it set off down the overgrown path. Not one of the knights noticed that the maiden was no longer following them, and before they became aware of the fact they had covered a league and more. As for the man who acted as her guard and escort, he kept but a poor watch on her: she had not even given him the slip, she simply wandered off without knowing where either track was leading.

The palfrey followed the path without straying to left or right, for it had trodden it many a time, winter and summer. The unhappy maiden, having started down it, kept looking around her for the knights and barons, but in vain; the forest was deep and dark and hazardous and she was dismayed at finding herself alone. It was no wonder she was frightened, and she could not help puzzling greatly as to where the assembled knights had vanished to. She was happy to have eluded them, but was upset and worried at having no company save that of God and the palfrey, which was no stranger to the path. She commended herself to God's keeping, and the dapple-grey palfrey carried her on. Dejected and anxious, she gave her mount its head, and never uttered a sound for fear the others should hear her and come back for her: to die in the wood was preferable to contracting such a marriage. Such were her thoughts as she rode along, and the palfrey, keen to get home by the familiar route, covered so much ground at its easy amble that it swiftly reached the perimeter of that great tract of woodland. At the foot of a slope a river flowed swift and dark. The grey palfrey, which knew the ford, headed straight towards it and lost no time in crossing over. They had not left its narrow shallows far behind, when, from the quarter the palfrey was making for, the maiden heard the sound of a horn. Above the main gate stood the watchman, heralding the dawn with trumpet blast.

The maiden rode straight towards the sound till she found herself beneath the castle, bewildered and distraught, like some errant soul who has lost his way and doesn't know how to ask it. The palfrey however, never faltering in its course, stepped on to the drawbridge which spanned a deep moat running right round the castle. The watchman blowing his horn above heard the clip-clop of the palfrey's hoofs on the bridge it had so often crossed. He stopped winding his horn and was silent for a while: then he climbed down from his look-out and called out sharply:

'Who comes riding so hard across the bridge at this hour?'

'Assuredly the most unhappy girl ever born of woman,' came

the answer. 'For God's sake let me come in until I see the dawn break, for I don't know where to go.'

'Damsel,' replied the other, 'you can take it for certain that I wouldn't dare to let you or anyone else enter this castle without my lord's leave. There was never a man in such distress as he is: his spirits are quite crushed, so cruelly has he been abused.'

While he was speaking of this he brought his eyes level with a judas in the postern gate. There was no need of a candle or lantern, for the moon was shining brightly. He saw the dapple-grey palfrey and recognized it all right, though he looked at it carefully first, much puzzled as to how it had got there. The maiden too, who was holding the reins, came under close scrutiny, in her rich attire and new, resplendent clothes. Then he scurried off to see his lord who was lying in bed in cheerless solitude.

'Sir,' he said, 'your pardon, but there's a woman all forlorn – young by her looks and splendidly apparelled, who has come out of the woods. Her garb is sumptuous: I think she is wearing a rich, furred cape, and her gown appears to be of the finest cloth. The young lady, who looks sad and woebegone, is seated on your dapple-grey palfrey. Her speech does her no injustice, on the contrary she is so pretty and gracious that, without exaggeration, sir, I don't believe there's another maid in the country to compare with her. If you ask me, she's a fairy sent here by God to compensate you for the injury which is weighing so heavily on your spirits. You have got fair value for the maiden you have lost.'

On hearing this Sir William sprang to his feet without waiting for more. Covered only with a surcoat he came running to the gate and had it quickly opened. The maiden called out to him in plaintive tones:

'Ah! noble knight, I have endured so much fatigue this night! For the love of God, sir, if it's no trouble to you, let me into your manor: I have no wish to tarry long, but I go in mortal fear of being pursued by certain knights who are very much alarmed at having lost me. I have come to ask your protection, chance having brought me here, for I have lost my way and am in dire distress.'

Sir William was overcome with joy at hearing her. He recognized the palfrey that had been so long in his stable, and he recognized the maiden, too, on sight, and I tell you truly that no happier man could possibly exist. He led her inside and lifted her down from her horse, and taking her right hand in his he kissed her more than twenty times, at which she made not the least demur, for she had recognized him too. The two of them were so delighted at seeing one another that they forgot all their woes. She was helped off with her cape, and they both sat down on a quilt of richest silk, edged with gold, and crossed themselves at least twenty times apiece, for they could hardly believe they were not dreaming. When there were no servants around they were not at a loss to solace themselves with kisses, but I assure you that no other impropriety took place on that occasion. The maiden recounted her adventure from beginning to end and swore that she must have been born under a lucky star for God to have brought her thither and delivered her, with only chance to guide her, from the clutches of her aged suitor, who was expecting a good return on his outlay of goods and money. When morning lightened Sir William went to attire himself. He had the maiden brought to his chapel within the walls and, sending for his chaplain on the spot, he got himself married without recall and joined in valid matrimony, whose bonds are not easily put asunder. And when mass had been sung, servants, waiting-maids and squires roistered and celebrated in the palace.

This outcome, though, was bound to be most unpalatable to those who had lost the maiden through their folly. They had arrived in a body at the lonely chapel, each and every one in a state of exhaustion and distress from the night-long ride. The ancient asked for his daughter, and the knight who had taken such poor care of her did not know what to say. He answered hurriedly:

'Sir, I put her in front of me and I rode behind, seeing that the track was very narrow and the forest murky and deep. I cannot tell if she took another direction, for I was drowsing on my saddle-bow; I woke up from time to time and thought she was still ahead of me, but now she is nowhere around and I don't know what has become of her; it's a poor watch we kept on her.'

The ancient sought her high and low, inquiring her whereabouts of everyone and asking whether they had seen her, but all were mystified and nobody could give him news of her. The old man who was to have married the maid was the most upset; he was not dilatory in seeking her, but it was a hopeless chase: he had no trail to follow. In the midst of this turmoil his companions sighted a squire coming up the track at the gallop; he rode straight up to the ancient and announced:

'My lord, Sir William assures you of his warm friendship. He married your daughter this very morning at dawn, to his great happiness and joy. You are to come over right away, my lord, and he invites his uncle, too, who played him false; he forgives him this injury now that your daughter is bestowed on him.'

The ancient took in this astonishing news, the like of which he had never heard. He shouted to all his barons to gather round, and when they were all assembled it was agreed that he should go and take with him the man to whom he had affianced his daughter. He saw his marriage plans in ruins, there was no possible redress. Thereupon this canny and hard-headed man betook himself thither in all haste, accompanied by his barons. On arriving at the house they met with a ceremonious welcome: Sir William received them with all the jubilation of a man delighted with his catch. Like it or not, the ancient was obliged to approve the marriage, and the wrinkled old uncle consoled himself as best he could.

Thus, my lords, did it please God that this marriage, which found favour in His sight, be lastingly established. Sir William was a sterling knight, as courtly as he was valorous; he never abandoned his pursuit of chivalry, but strove even harder for renown, winning the friendship of counts and princes. Within three years, according to the tale, the ancient died, leaving Sir William all he had. So the latter found himself holding lands worth a good thousand pounds a year, and administered justice throughout the great and well-defended domain. Death claimed his powerful uncle next, and William, who was no simpleton, nor of a mean or craven nature, nor given to speaking ill of his neighbours, added his uncle's lands to his, unchallenged by any. And so this tale that I have rhymed I now conclude in accordance with the true facts of the story.

THE COUNT OF PONTIEU'S DAUGHTER

Introduction

IF *The Count of Pontieu's Daughter* is, as seems probable, older than *Aucassin and Nicolette*, then it can claim to be in its original version the first Old French tale to have been written in prose. Only one manuscript now remains, written in a late-thirteenth-century hand, though a second is also known to have existed. That the legend enjoyed a certain popularity is proved by the existence of two later versions, the first incorporated in the *Histoire d'outre mer et du roi Saladin*, a largely fictional chronicle compiled in the mid thirteenth century, the second forming part of the fifteenth-century *Roman de Jean d'Avesnes*. Around 1660 a misguided attempt was made to furnish the characters with historical prototypes, and the renewal of interest in the rediscovered text resulted over the years in one novel, two operas and a five-act tragedy. The later versions are both derived from the one translated here and are not, by any standards, improvements on it. The bare bones of the story acquire successive layers of padding, the element of suspense is done away with and clumsy attempts to explain the characters' motivation merely succeed in dissipating the ambiguity which chiefly holds the reader's interest.

The tale has many of the features of the *conte populaire* (the peccant wife consigned to the waves in a barrel, families sundered and reunited in foreign parts, the failure to recognize one's kith and kin), and indeed it is a sort of fairy tale in a naturalistic setting. The author has clearly gone out of his way to give it an air of realism by locating it in what was probably his own home territory, the northernmost corner of France. The characters are given the titles of well-known local families, the places mentioned are concentrated in that area, or else are such as would, in the wake of the Crusades, have become household names. None the less in its manner of telling it is reminiscent of the folk-tale and its laconic style contrasts strangely with the explicitness of the other works where every 'i' is dotted and every 't' crossed. The mood is matter-of-fact, the prose almost stark in its simplicity. Events which might rightly be considered remarkable, not to say fantastic, are narrated in so impassive a way that eyebrows remain firmly in their place. Yet the author was no novice at his craft. His technique is much less artless than it might appear and he has, in fact, suited his style to his matter with an admirable sense of what was wanted.

The story might be called an exercise in non-communication, for not only is the author parsimonious with his comments, leaving much to be deduced or read between the lines, but the characters themselves are quite remarkably reticent in their dealings with one another. No better antithesis could be found to the conversational elegancies in which Renart's knight and lady take such delight than the austere and almost monosyllabic dignity of these exchanges. Indeed the whole crux of the story hangs upon this failure in communication; and having taken the '*remanieurs*' to task for destroying the suspense I now find myself faced with committing the self-same blunder by summarizing the story, if I am to discuss its moral implications. Hence any reader with a respect for the author's narrative skills would do well to skip what follows.

Sir Theobald, a poor knight with expectations, marries the daughter of the neighbouring Count of Pontieu. The marriage is happy but childless, and after some years the disappointed couple decide to invoke the help of St James of Compostella. *En route* they fall a prey to brigands who bind the knight hand and foot and violate the lady before making off with their booty. Instead of setting her husband free, as he requests, the lady snatches up a sword and tries to kill him, but only succeeds in cutting through his bonds, whereupon she compounds the injury by expressing regret at having failed in her purpose. On their return her indignant father takes her out to sea and puts her overboard in a barrel. Saved by some passing merchants, she is carried off to Almeria and sold to the sultan, who marries her willy-nilly, and to whom she bears two children. The count her father, troubled by remorse, sets out for the Holy Land with his son-in-law and son. A storm on their homeward journey blows them into Almeria. The lady recognizes them and begs their lives from the sultan. She makes them tell their story and when they come to the point where Sir Theobald's wife attempted to murder him she breaks in with the words: 'I know why she wanted to kill him.' 'Madam, why?' 'Because of the terrible shame he had seen her suffer and be subjected to before his eyes.' 'Alas, where was her guilt therein?' cried the wretched husband, adding: 'I swear I would never have looked on her less fondly on that account.' 'Sir,' comes the reply, 'that was not her belief at the time.' The resourceful lady then proceeds to hoodwink the sultan and make her escape with the three men, taking her son by the sultan with her. The Pope straightens out the matrimonial tangle and they all return to Pontieu amid general rejoicing.

So far, so good, but a closer look reveals that much is left unsaid. Why exactly did she wish to kill him? It has been suggested, and the later versions tend in this direction without ever going so far, that she loved her husband too much to bear the thought of his living with the memory of her shame. Or, more plausibly, that she was so out of her mind with anguish that she wished to eliminate the witness of her degradation. But primitive societies imputed responsibility to the woman who suffered outrage, whatever the circumstances, and it seems likely that the legend embodies a survival of this crude justice. Following the principle that dead men tell no tales, the lady was therefore making sure that she would not be made to pay a second time. This seems to tally better with what she eventually says than theories crediting her with over-delicate sentiments. Sir Theobald, however, was not dead and did tell tales. Was it with malice aforethought, or did the duke worm it out of his reluctant son-in-law? Both have been argued. I think the truth may lie somewhere in between: he could not bring himself to keep it quiet, and yet he did not actually relish spilling the beans – a very human failing. Certainly, as is also frequent, he regretted having done so. On the whole he comes out of it much better than his lady, who was assuredly wise in her generation and whose watchword should have been expediency. She shows remarkably little scruple in cheating the trusting but somewhat naïve sultan, but then he was an infidel, so perhaps it did not count. And she hedges her bets, too, to the very last, which may explain why, on her return, she lived out her life in strict penance, while Sir

Theobald merely 'lived and died a good and worthy man'. Conscience caught up with her in the end.

One of the chief attractions of the tale is that it leaves so many loose ends for the reader to amuse himself tying up as the fancy takes him. The story is at once moral and amoral. The characters all pay for their sins in one way or another, except the sultan, who pays for other people's. But how convenient that the lady's brother should mysteriously die in the penultimate chapter, thus ensuring a double inheritance to Sir Theobald's sons! And was the birth of those sons due to a belated intervention on St James's part? Or was it perhaps an indirect legacy of the lady's years as a sultana? The reader must decide.

EDITIONS

La Fille du Comte de Pontieu, ed. Clovis Brunel, S.A.T.F., Paris, 1923 (contains all three versions together with a lengthy introduction).

La Fille du Comte de Pontieu, nouvelle du xiii⁰ siècle, ed. Clovis Brunel, Classiques Français du Moyen Age, Paris, 1926 (omits the fifteenth-century version).

There is also an interpretative study by E. Winkler in *Zeitschrift für romanische Philologie*, XLIV, 1925, p. 340.

The Count of Pontieu's Daughter

[1] There was in time past a count of Pontieu, who dearly loved this life. In those same days the Count of Saint-Pol was an ageing man; he had no direct heir, but he had a sister who was the lady of Domart in Pontieu. This lady had a son called Theobald, who was heir to the county of Saint-Pol, but during his uncle's lifetime lived as a poor squire. The Count of Pontieu had an excellent lady to wife who bore him a daughter, and this daughter grew and flourished in health and weal and attained her seventeenth year; her mother, however, died before she was three years old and the count remarried soon after. Within a short time he had a son who lived to thrive and prosper.

[2] The Count of Pontieu saw Sir Theobald and took him into his household, and during his time of service the count's emprises met with great success. On returning one day from a tournament the count called Sir Theobald over and inquired of him:

'Theobald, what jewel of my land would you like best?'

'Sir,' replied Theobald, 'I am a poor squire, but of all the jewels of your land there is none I should like so well as your lady daughter.'

The count was delighted and said:

'Theobald, I will give her to you if she will have you.'

The count went to find his daughter and said to her:

'Daughter, you are married, provided you make no demur.'

'Sir,' she inquired, 'to whom?'

'Daughter, to my good knight Theobald of Domart.'

'Ah, sir,' she replied, 'if your county were a kingdom and all were to be mine, I should consider myself well portioned in marrying him!'

'A blessing, daughter, on your heart's liking!' exclaimed the count.

[3] The marriage was celebrated. The counts of Pontieu and

Saint-Pol were present, along with a large and joyous gathering of worthy barons. The couple enjoyed five years of perfect happiness together, but, to their mutual chagrin, it was not God's pleasure that they should have an heir. One night as Sir Theobald lay in bed he thought to himself:

'God! how is it that I and this lady love one another so dearly, and yet are unable to have a son who would serve God and work for the world's weal.'

He bethought himself of the great St James who granted the prayers of such as truly invoked his help, and vowed that he would go on a pilgrimage to his shrine. His lady was asleep, and when she awoke he took her in his arms and asked a boon of her.

'What is it, sir?' she inquired.

'Madam, is it certain that you will grant it me?'

'Sir, let me hear it, and whatever it is I will grant it you so be I can.'

'Madam, it's leave I want to go on a pilgrimage to my lord St James's shrine, and I will pray to the good saint to give us an heir who will serve God and honour Holy Church.'

'Sir,' she replied, 'that is indeed a seemly boon and I grant it you.'

Both were deeply happy. One day went by, and another, and the next, and that night as they were lying together in bed the lady said:

'Sir, I have a request to make of you.'

'Ask, madam, and I will grant it you if I can.'

'Sir,' she said, 'I ask your leave to go with you on this pilgrimage.'

Sir Theobald was very upset at hearing this, and said:

'Madam, it would be an arduous journey for you.'

'Sir, never doubt that the least of your squires will be more of a nuisance to you than ever I shall be.'

'Madam,' he said, 'you have my consent.'

Morning came, and the news spread till it reached the ears of the Count of Pontieu, who sent for Sir Theobald and said to him:

'Well, Theobald, I hear that you are a sworn pilgrim, and my daughter too?'

'Sir, it's the truth.'

'Theobald, in your case I am pleased and in hers sorry.'

'Sir,' he replied, 'I cannot refuse her.'

'Then, Theobald, set out when you will and make haste. I will provide you with plenty of palfreys and cobs and pack-horses, and other necessities.'

'Sir, I thank you kindly,' answered Sir Theobald.

[4] He made his preparations and set out joyfully, and rode on his way till he was less than two days' journey from St James's shrine. He spent the night in a goodly town and that evening he summoned the innkeeper and asked him what tomorrow's ride would be like.

'Sir,' answered the other, 'a little beyond this town you will have to pass through a stretch of woodland; but afterwards it's good going all the way.'

No more was said. The bed was made ready and they went to rest. Next morning was fine and the pilgrims were up and stirring before dawn. Sir Theobald woke and, feeling a little out of sorts, said to his chamberlain:

'Get up and rouse our people, and get them loaded up and under way, and you, stay behind and pack up our things, for I am feeling rather low and out of sorts.'

The chamberlain gave the order and the household set out. Sir Theobald himself rose shortly after, the servant packed the baggage, the palfreys were harnessed and the three of them mounted; it was not yet dawn, but the weather was fine and clear. The trio rode out of town with no other company save that of God, and were soon approaching the forest where two tracks, one well-trodden and the other rough, led away into the woodland. Sir Theobald spoke to the chamberlain saying:

'Spur on and catch our people up, and tell them to wait for us. It is very ill-advised for a lady to ride through forested country without a proper escort.'

He galloped off and Sir Theobald, riding up to the forest's verge, came upon these two tracks; not knowing which to choose he said to the lady:

'Madam, which road shall we take?'

'Please God, sir, the good one,' she replied.

Now there were robbers in the forest who used to tread the wrong road smooth on purpose to mislead the pilgrims. Sir Theobald dismounted and examined the way ahead, and found the wrong road wider and more frequented than the right.

'Madam,' he said, 'in God's name let us take this one.'

They set off along it and had covered a good quarter of a league when the track began to grow narrow, with overhanging branches.

'Madam,' said Sir Theobald then, 'it seems to me that we are badly astray.'

[5] Hardly had he said this when he spied four men ahead of him, armed in the fashion of robbers, each on a big horse and carrying a lance. As soon as he caught sight of them he glanced behind him and seeing four more, similarly equipped, he said:

'Madam, be not alarmed at anything you see.'

He hailed the first group, and his greeting was met with silence. Next he asked them what their intentions towards him were, and one of them answered:

'You will soon find out!' and with that he had at him with his lance, thinking to pierce him through the body, but Sir Theobald saw the blow coming and ducked in alarm and the robber missed him, while Sir Theobald grabbed hold of the lance as he passed and wrenched it out of his grasp. Thereupon he spurred at the group from which his assailant had come and killed one of them with a thrust through the body. Then wheeling round, he dashed back on his tracks and transfixed his first attacker, dropping him dead. So it was that, God willing, he killed three out of the eight before the remaining five surrounded him and felled his palfrey; he bit the dust then, but came to no serious harm. He had no sword or other weapon with which he might have defended himself. They stripped him to his shirt, divesting him of gown and spurs and breeches, and taking a sword-belt they bound him hand and foot and threw him into a bramble thicket. Having disposed of him they went to the lady and took her palfrey and gown, leaving her in her shift. She was very beautiful, albeit she was weeping bitterly. One of the robbers looked at her and said:

'Sirs, I have lost my brother, and I want this lady in compensation.'

Another said:

'And I've lost my first cousin, I've got as good a claim as you.'

The third and fourth said likewise; and the fifth said to them:

'Sirs, detaining her won't benefit us much, so let us take her into the wood and have our will of her, and then set her on the road again and let her go.'

And so they did, and brought her back to the track.

[6] Sir Theobald saw her and called out:

'Madam, unloose me, for God's sake, these briars are hurting me cruelly!'

The lady caught sight of one of the dead robbers' swords lying on the ground and, picking it up, she approached Sir Theobald with the words:

'Sir, I will set you free all right!'

She thought to run him through the body, but he saw the blow coming and, seized with fear, performed a wild contortion which landed him with his back and hands uppermost, so that as she struck she wounded him in the arms and severed the straps that bound him. Feeling his hands free, he drew them to him at once and, breaking his bonds, jumped to his feet exclaiming:

'Madam, so it please God, you will not kill me today!'

To which she replied:

'Indeed, sir, and that grieves me.'

He took the sword away from her and, laying his hand on her shoulder, he led her back the way they had come.

[7] On arriving at the forest's edge he found the main body of his party gathered there. When his people saw him stripped of clothing they cried out:

'Sir, who ever reduced you to such a state?'

He told them that they had met with robbers who had subjected them to this treatment; his companions were sorry to hear it, but soon had them arrayed again, and they all mounted and set out afresh. Never once during the day's ride did Sir Theobald treat his wife with less than his usual courtesy. They put up for the night in a sizeable town where Sir Theobald asked the innkeeper if there were a convent near by where one might leave a lady.

'Sir, you are in luck,' replied the landlord, 'there is a very godly establishment next door.'

The night passed and in the morning Sir Theobald went to the convent and heard mass. Afterwards he requested the abbess to keep his lady safe against his return, and she agreed. He left some of his people to wait on her and continued his journey. His pilgrimage completed, he called on his way back, gave alms to the convent and reclaimed his wife, whom he took back home again with as great a show of joy and honour as at their setting out, save that he did not sleep in her bed.

[8] On returning to his country he met with a splendid welcome. The Count of Pontieu was there, and also his uncle the Count of Saint-Pol, and their ladies and maidens paid great honour to his wife. That day the Count of Pontieu had Sir Theobald eat from his own dish. After the meal he said to him:

'Theobald, my dear son, those who fare far afield see sights; so tell me some adventure that you saw or heard about.'

Sir Theobald answered that he knew of no adventure he could relate, but on the count's pressing him a second time he said:

'Sir, since the tale must out, I won't tell it you in the hearing of such a crowd.'

The count rose and, taking him by the hand, led him aside, and Sir Theobald told him how it had happened thus and thus to a certain knight and lady, but without mentioning any names. The count asked him what the knight had done with the lady, and Sir Theobald answered that he had brought her home with as great a show of joy and honour as at their faring forth, save that he did not sleep in her bed.

'Theobald, that knight was of another mind than I, for, by the faith I owe you, had I been in his place I would have hanged her from the branch of a tree by her braids or a briar stem or the leather strap itself!'

'Sir,' said Sir Theobald, 'then the story would not have carried nearly as much conviction as it will when the lady herself bears witness to its truth.'

'Theobald,' said the count, 'do you know who the knight was?'

'Sir, I do indeed.'

'Who was he?' asked the other.

'Sir, it was I.'

'It was my daughter then who acted thus?'

'Yes, sir, it was.'

'Theobald,' said the count, 'in bringing her back to me you have ensured your being well avenged.'

Grim with anger he summoned the lady and asked her if it were true, what Sir Theobald had told him.

'What's that?' she asked.

'That you attempted to kill him as he says.'

'Yes, sir,' she replied.

'But why did you want to do it?'

'Sir,' she replied, 'for a reason that makes me still regret my not having done so.'

[9] The count left it at that and let the court disperse, but on the second day he took Sir Theobald and his son to the coast at Rue, and had the lady brought along as well. The count had a big, sea-worthy boat made ready, and had the lady put aboard, along with a barrel, and fire, and pitch, and the three men too got into the boat, unaccompanied by any save the mariners who sailed it. The count bade them put out to sea, and when they had covered some two leagues he had one of the ends knocked out of the barrel and had the lady, in all her beauty and fine apparel, put into the butt; then he had the end wedged back on top of her and caulked with pitch, and the bung securely replaced to make it watertight, and with that the barrel was heaved at his order on to the side of the ship, whence he himself kicked it overboard, commending it to wind and waves. Sir Theobald and the lady's brother were seized with horror and fell at his feet, begging him, for God's sake, to let them save her from this cruel agony, but he was adamant.

[10] However, the count had not yet reached the shore when a merchant ship came sailing along from Flanders, heading for

Saracen shores for purposes of trade. The mariners sighted the floating cask and one of them called out:

'Look, there's an empty barrel! It might come in useful if we had it on board.'

The speaker was sent to fetch it in and they got it on board the ship. On examining it they observed that the bottom was newly caulked, so they knocked it in and found the lady lying inside and clearly about to expire for want of air, her neck distended, her face swollen and her eyes revulsed. Out in the air again she drew a deep gasping breath. The merchants who were standing round spoke to her urgently, but she was unable to utter a word. However, as the breath returned to her body she regained the power of speech and talked to them. They asked her who she was, but she hid the truth from them, telling them that a cruel fate and dreadful crime had brought her to this pass. After she had eaten and drunk the swelling subsided and she regained her beauty, and the joy and relief she felt equalled her former anguish.

[11] The ship sailed on until it arrived off Almeria. When they had entered the harbour galleys came out to accost them and ask them who they were, to which they replied:

'We are merchants.'

They had warrants from those in authority enabling them to voyage where they would in safety. They went ashore, taking the lady with them, and asked one another what they had best do with her. One suggested that they sell her, while another said:

'If my advice were followed we would present her to the Sultan of Almeria, our business will go all the better for it.'

They all agreed to this and, taking the lady, they led her to the sultan – a youngish man – and offered her as a prize; he received her with alacrity, for she was a lady of outstanding beauty. On the sultan's asking who she was, the merchants answered that they did not know and explained how they had found her: The sultan treated the merchants generously and, as for the lady, he held her more than dear. Once she was on dry land the colour returned to her cheeks, quickening love and desire in the sultan's heart. He had an interpreter inquire of her what lineage she came of, but never a word would she vouchsafe. He felt sure from her appearance and demeanour that she was a lady of high birth and had the interpreter ask her if she was a Christian, adding that if she would renounce her religion he would take her to wife. Seeing clearly that it would be better for her to bow to love than to duress, she sent him word that she would do so. The sultan married her when she had abjured her faith and loved her with increasing ardour, and she had not been long with him when she conceived and bore a son. She mixed freely with his people and spoke and understood the pagan tongue. Not long afterwards she had a daughter. She lived thus for some two and a half years with the sultan and understood the language and spoke it fluently.

[12] The count, meanwhile, was in Pontieu, according to the tale, as were his son and Sir Theobald too. The count was sunk in gloom, Sir Theobald durst not marry again, and the count's son, seeing those he loved in such tribulation, was loth to become a knight, although he was well of an age to do so. One day that the count was much haunted in mind by the sin he had committed against his daughter he betook himself to the archbishop of Rouen, made his confession and took the cross. When Sir Theobald learned that his good lord the count had taken the cross, he too made his confession and did likewise; and the count's son, seeing his father and his much-loved brother Sir Theobald wearing the crusader's badge, in his turn took the cross. When the count his father saw what the lad had done he was much concerned and said:

'Good son, why have you taken the cross? There will be no one now to guard and govern the land.'

But his son replied:

'Dear father, I have taken the cross to serve God and yourself.'

The count made his preparations and set out on his journey. He and Sir Theobald and the youth arrived in the Holy Land without hurt to life or limb or chattels. They made their pilgrimage with great devotion, visiting every place where they learned that God was to be served. And when the count had done that much he felt that he would like to do still more, and offered his services and those of his companions to the Knights Templar for a twelvemonth.

When the year was up he felt a wish to see his land and his friends once more, so he sent orders to Acre for a ship to be made ready and, bidding farewell to the Holy Land, he journeyed to Acre and there embarked.

[13] It was with a fair wind abaft that they left the port of Acre, but it did not favour them long. Once they were on the high seas an ugly storm sprang up, so wild that the mariners completely lost their bearings. Thinking each hour would be their last, the three men roped themselves together, the son to the father, kith to kin. Indeed, they lashed themselves so fast that there was no parting them. They had not voyaged far in that fashion when they sighted land; on their asking what the country was, they were told that it was Saracen territory, a country called Almeria, and the mariners inquired of them:

'Sirs, what is your pleasure?'

'Sail on,' replied the count, 'we can't meet a worse end than death by drowning.'

Their ship was a near wreck when they drifted into Almeria. Galleys and small craft crowded with Saracens came out to meet them, and they were taken captive and led before the sultan and all their wealth and chattels presented to him as booty. The sultan disbanded the crew and sent them to his dungeons. The count and his sons were still so tightly lashed together that it proved impossible to part them, so the sultan ordered them to be put in a cell apart. There they mouldered for some time in conditions of great hardship, and the count's son fell gravely ill.

[14] There came a day when the Sultan of Almeria made a great feast to celebrate his birthday. Guests thronged the court, and after the banquet archers and Turkish men-at-arms presented themselves before the ruler with the request:

'Sire, we demand our customary right.'

'What's that?' he asked.

'A captive, sire, to serve as target.'

'Go to the dungeons,' he replied, 'and pick the one who has least time to live.'

Off they went and seized the count and brought him out,

decked in his matted beard and straggling locks and precious little beside. The sultan said to them:

'This man was not fit for longer living. Go on, take him away.'

The lady who was wife to the sultan was present at the time, and the sight of the captive moved her heart to pity.

'Sir,' she said, 'I know French and would speak with this poor man, if it were your pleasure.'

'By all means, madam,' he replied.

She approached the man and asked him whence he hailed and who he was.

'Madam,' he replied, 'I come from a part of France, a country called Pontieu.'

'And from what lineage?'

'Madam, I was lord and count of the country when I left it.'

When she heard this she returned to her lord and said:

'Sir, give me this captive if it be your pleasure, for he knows how to play at chess and at tric-trac, and can play before us and teach us. Also I am rather lonely here and he will be company for me.'

'Madam, by the faith that I profess, I grant it gladly.'

She sent the captive to her chamber, and the jailer went back to the dungeon and brought out Sir Theobald, with nothing but his hair and beard to cover his gaunt, emaciated body.

When the lady saw him she said again:

'Sir, I would speak with this one too, if you have no objection.'

'None, madam, by my faith.'

So the lady approached Sir Theobald and asked him also whence he hailed and who he was.

'Madam, I am from the old man's country; I am a knight and married his daughter.'

She went back to her lord and said to him:

'Sir, you will be doing me a great favour if you grant me the life of this captive, for he is well versed in every pastime, and you would enjoy watching the two of them play together.'

'Madam,' he said, 'he is yours.'

The archers grew impatient and said:

'Sire, we are being made to wait too long for our due right.'

Next it was the turn of the son to be fetched out of the dungeon and led up; he was beardless and his splendid shock of hair was his only covering, and so extreme was his weakness that he could hardly stand. The sight of him moved the lady to pity, and she said:

'Sir, is it your pleasure that I speak with this man too?'

'Yes indeed, madam.'

Going up to him, she asked him who he was and whom he served.

'Madam,' he answered, 'I am son to the first old man.'

On hearing this she said to her lord:

'Sir, you will be doing me a great favour in giving me this youth as well, for he knows chess and tric-trac and has a great stock of fine tales.'

'By my faith, madam,' said the sultan, 'were there a hundred of them, I would give them to you gladly!'

The lady sent him to join the two others, while the soldiers returned to the dungeons and fetched yet another captive. She spoke to this man too, but did not know him, and he was delivered up to his martyrdom.

[15] As soon as ever she could the lady left the gathering and went to the chamber where her prisoners were waiting. When they saw her coming they attempted to rise, but she gestured to them to sit still. As she drew near the count asked her:

'Madam, when will they kill us?'

'Not yet awhile,' she replied.

'More's the pity, madam,' said the count, 'for hunger has brought us to the brink of collapse.'

At that the lady went away and had some meat prepared, which she brought to them, carving it with her own hand before giving each man a morsel and a drop to drink. This bite of nourishment left them even more famished than before. She fed them thus ten times that day, a morsel or two at a time. That night they slept in comfort. And so for eight days the lady fed and nourished them with measured helpings, until they were strong enough for her to allow them unrestricted access to food and drink. They were given chess sets and tric-trac too, which they played among themselves, basking in their well-being. The sultan took pleasure in coming to watch them play; as for the lady, she kept such a careful watch over herself while in their company that her true identity never once struck the eyes or crossed the mind of any one of them.

[16] It was not long after that the sultan had trouble on his hands: a neighbouring caliph laid his lands to waste and he sent out a general summons, preparing to avenge himself. When the lady learned what was afoot she betook herself to the chamber where her prisoners spent their days; they had grown so used to her presence that they made no move to rise either when she entered or left the room. She sat down on a chair in front of them and addressed them, saying:

'Sirs, you gave me some information concerning yourselves, and I want to find out now if what you said to me was true. You told me that you were count of Pontieu, that this man married your daughter and that the youth here is your son. I am a Saracen and familiar with the magic arts, and I swear to you that you were never within range of so shameful a death as threatens you now if you do not tell me the truth, and I shall know all right if you speak true or not. Your daughter, whom this man married, what became of her?'

'Madam,' replied the count, 'I believe her to be dead.'

'How did she come to die?' asked the lady.

'Madam,' he answered, 'for a sufficient reason, well-deserved.'

'What was that reason?'

The count embarked on the story of the marriage and told her of how the couple had waited in vain for an heir. The good knight, he said, undertook to go on a pilgrimage to St James's shrine, she asked to accompany him and he agreed, and they set out on their journey. There came a stage where they were unescorted and met with robbers in a forest. The good knight could not prevail against so many, and though he killed three, there remained five who overpowered him and stripped him to his shirt, and his lady too. Afterwards they bound him hand and foot and threw him into a bramble thicket. Seeing the lady's beauty, each of them wanted to possess her, and they agreed among themselves that all five of them would lie with her. Having taken their will of her, they went off, leaving her where she was. The good knight saw her and spoke to her very gently, saying: 'Madam, loose my bonds and we will go on our way.' She spied a sword that one of the robbers had let fall and, picking it up, approached him with a wild and baleful look, saying: 'I will set you free all right!' Holding the naked blade aloft she thought to run him through the body, but by the will of God and his own strength the good knight rolled right over, so that she struck the bonds, severing them and wounding him in the arms. His hands freed he broke the bonds round his ankles and, despite his wounds, jumped to his feet with the words: 'Madam, so it please God, you will not kill me today!' To which she replied: 'That grieves me!'

'Ah!' exclaimed the lady. 'I know you have spoken the truth, and I know too why she wanted to kill him.'

'Madam, why?'

'Because of the terrible shame he had seen her suffer and be subjected to before his eyes.'

These words moved Sir Theobald to tears and he said, weeping:

'Alas! where was her guilt therein? Madam,' he added, 'as I hope God will deliver me from my captivity, I swear I would never have looked on her less fondly on that account.'

'Sir,' she replied, 'that was not her belief at the time.'

[17] 'But tell me now,' she said, 'which were better, in your opinion, that she were alive or dead?'

'Madam,' they answered, 'that we do not know.'

'But I do know,' added the count, 'that the vengeance wreaked on her was a cruel one.'

'And if it had been God's pleasure that she should escape from that torment, and if you could have news of her, what would you say then?'

'Madam,' replied the count, 'it would give me greater joy than my deliverance from this captivity and the holding of twice the lands I ever had!'

'As for me, madam,' said Sir Theobald, 'the loveliest lady in the world and the kingdom of France to boot would not make me as happy!'

'Verily, madam,' said the youth, 'nothing that I could be given or promised would fill me with such joy!'

The lady's heart grew tender as she listened to their assurances.

'God be praised!' she exclaimed. 'Now mind there is no deceit in what you say.'

The three replied with a single voice:

'Madam, there is none.'

The lady began to weep with deeply felt emotion.

'Then, sirs, you may now say that you are my father and I your daughter, and you my lord, and you my brother.'

These words saw them the happiest of men, and they would have bowed down low before her, but she stopped them, saying:

'I am a Saracen, and therefore I beg you not to let your joy at what you have heard reflect itself in your bearing; just behave with simplicity and leave everything to me. I will tell you now why I made myself known to you. My lord the sultan is to set out on a campaign; I know you well and will ask that you be allowed to accompany him, and if ever you were men of valour show it now!'

No more was said, and the lady rose and went to make her request to the sultan.

'Sir, one of my prisoners has heard about your war and has told me that he would gladly ride with you, if he had leave to do so.'

'Madam,' replied the sultan, 'I would not dare, for fear he should play me false.'

'Sir,' she said, 'you can grant him leave with perfect safety, for I will keep the other two, and if this man did you any wrong I would hang the others by the neck.'

'Then, madam, I will provide him with a horse and arms and whatever he will need.'

With that the lady returned to the chamber and said:

'Sir, you will ride with the sultan.'

Her brother fell at her feet and implored her:

'For the love of God, sister, arrange for me to go too!'

'That you shall not,' she said, 'it would make the business too obvious.'

[18] The sultan set out, Sir Theobald in his retinue, and they came upon their enemies. The sultan furnished him with everything he needed. By the will of God, and in another's interest, Sir Theobald performed such prodigies that in a short space he had discomfited the sultan's foes. The sultan conceived a great liking for him, and after riding home victorious with a throng of prisoners in his train he went to the lady and said to her:

'Madam, by the creed that I profess, I have nothing but praise for your prisoner. I would certainly grant him a great domain if such was his desire.'

'Sir,' she answered, 'he would not accept it without good reason.'

They spoke no more of it: meanwhile she prepared her scheme.

'Sir,' she said, 'I am with child and am unwell.'

'Madam,' said the sultan, 'the two-fold increase of my realm would not make me so happy a man!'

'Sir,' she went on, 'nothing I have eaten or drunk has had any savour for me since you went away, and my old prisoner said to me that if I did not sojourn in a healthy country I should die.'

'Madam, your death is the last thing I desire; do but tell me what country you wish to go to and I will have you taken there.'

'Sir, I care not where it be, so long as I get off this island.'

The sultan had a splendid ship fitted out and furnished it with wine and meat.

'Sir,' said the lady then, 'I will take my old prisoner and the youth with me, I can watch them play at chess and tric-trac, and I will take my son along for solace and amusement.'

'And what will become of the third prisoner, madam?' asked the sultan. 'I had sooner you took him than the other two, for there is nowhere on land or sea where he will not defend you, should the need arise.'

'Then, sir, I am quite agreeable to taking him.'

The ship was equipped and manned and they put out to sea. No sooner were they on the high seas than the mariners announced to the lady:

'The wind we've got is carrying us straight to Brindisi.'

'Run on before the breeze,' she ordered, 'for I know French and will ensure your safety wherever you go.'

[19] They made harbour safely and went ashore. The lady then said to her companions:

'Sirs, I want you to remember the words that passed between us, for I am still quite free to return if I wish.'

'Madam,' they answered, 'we said nothing that we do not intend to abide by.'

'Sirs,' she said next, 'you see my son here. What shall we do with him?'

'Madam, may his coming greatly redound to his welfare and honour!'

'Sirs,' she said again, 'I have robbed the sultan of much in depriving him of my person and his son, and I have no wish to deprive him of anything else that is his.'

So saying, she returned to the ship and spoke to the mariners:

'Put back and tell the sultan that I have taken my person and his son away from him, and have released my father and my husband and my brother from his custody.'

The mariners were much dismayed to hear it, and set sail for home as soon as they could.

[20] The count fitted himself out, procuring the wherewithal from merchants and from the Templars, who gladly made him advances out of their funds. When all was ready they left the town and made their way to Rome. The count presented himself with his party before the Pope. Each member made his confession to him, and when the Pope had heard the burden of their story he rejoiced at the miraculous works that God had wrought in his time. He baptized the boy, who was given the name of William, and subsequently received the lady back into the Church and confirmed her and her lord in valid matrimony, finally giving each one a penance to perform for his misdeeds. These matters completed, they took to their horses and arrived at length amid great jubilation in the land of their birth, where they had been sorely missed and where they were met with joyful celebrations.

[21] The ship sailed out of Brindisi, returning to Almeria, where the mariners made their report, to the sultan's chagrin and profound displeasure. Never again did he feel the same love for the daughter

who had stayed behind; nevertheless she grew and developed into a girl of surpassing beauty.

[22] Back in Pontieu once again, the count knighted his son. In the succeeding period the youth's affairs prospered greatly, but he did not live long thereafter. At a great feast attended by the Count of Pontieu there was present a certain nobleman of Normandy, called Sir Raoul of Préaux. This Raoul had a very lovely daughter, and by dint of much parleying the count arranged a marriage between his nephew William and the daughter, the afore-named Sir Raoul having no other heir. William married her and in time became lord of Préaux. There was great rejoicing throughout the land, and Sir Theobald, by God's grace, had two sons of his wife. The count's son died, deeply mourned by all, but the Count of Saint-Pol was still alive, so the sons of Sir Theobald were in line for the two counties, to which they eventually acceded. The good lady lived out her life in strict penance and Sir Theobald lived and died a good and worthy man.

[23] It so happened that the daughter who had stayed behind with the sultan grew into a very beautiful maid and became known as the Fair Captive. There was in the sultan's service a brave and noble Turk called Malakin of Baghdad. The sight of this lovely creature awakened his desire and led him to say to the sultan:

'Sire, to ensure my being ever at your service, grant me a boon.'

'What boon, Malakin?'

'Sire, if I were not afraid to utter it, on account of my being of far humbler birth than she, I would tell you.'

'Speak with impunity,' declared the sultan.

'Sire, your daughter, the Fair Captive.'

'Malakin, I will give her to you gladly.'

The sultan gave him his daughter, and he married her and took her back to his country where she was received with the greatest joy and honour, and, as the truth is witness, to her was born the mother of the chivalrous Saladin.

THE CHATELAINE OF VERGY

Introduction

THIS story offers the combination of a romantic plot and a classical perfection in the art of composition. The exterior trappings of the story, the habiliments in which the timeless emotions of love, jealousy, suspicion and the rest are decked out and presented to us, are wholly of their time; indeed the work is among the most faithful illustrations of the courtly ethic. This is doubtless what endeared it to the public of its day: it was blessedly familiar, it consecrated a way of life and thought which many considered to be the ultimate goal to which a person of refinement might aspire; it did not have that slightly irreverent smirk worn by the works of Jean Renart which might displease the serious-minded; and at the same time it imposed on the familiar the stamp of the absolute. That this was recognized at the time of its writing is plain from the large number of manuscripts that survive. There remain some twenty of the poem in its original version, of which one, dating from 1288, gives us the *terminus ad quem* (the work itself may have been written at any time during the half century preceding). The fact that it spoke to and for a contemporary public would explain its popularity at that period, but only some universal quality in the situation and the characters involved can account for its continuing success, the frequent allusions to it by fourteenth- and fifteenth-century writers, the proliferation of updated versions in different centuries and countries.*

The Chatelaine of Vergy sees the return of tragedy to the courtly romance. It is akin in theme and spirit to another well-known work of the same period: the *Histoire du Chastelain de Couci et de la Dame de Fayel*. Since the appearance of the earliest version of the Tristan legend nearly a century before the wheel has come full circle. In the intervening years poets, strangely obsessed with this story and the problems it posed, had devoted their energies to removing

---

* A noteworthy example is to be found in the seventieth *nouvelle* of Marguerite of Navarre's *Heptameron*.

obstacles from true love's path (having mostly put them there in the first place), and above all to finding an acceptable solution to the plight of the girl who, already in love with one man, is committed to marrying another. Countless romances, from Chrétien's *Cligès* onwards, are built around that situation and forced to body forth the axiom '*qui a le cuer, si ait le cors*', no matter what the cost in verisimilitude. Only the *Conte de la Charrette* and, much more so, the Prose *Lancelot* come to terms, however equivocally, with adultery and suggest its tragic implications. Yet tragedy, as a possibility, lies at the very heart of courtly love, and the later writers, weary perhaps of a worked-out vein, were merely putting into romance form the situation typified in the lyric, and doubtless acted out often enough in life, though usually, one trusts, with consequences less macabre than those that overtake these fictional couples.

The traditional elements in this tale are already found in certain *lais* of Marie de France, notably in *Lanval* and in *Guingamor* with which our anonymous author was certainly familiar: the condition of absolute secrecy imposed on the lover by the lady (in Marie's poems a fay), and the advances made by the suzerain's wife to an unwilling vassal and his subsequent traducing to his lord. An attempt was made at one stage to identify the characters with certain historical personages of the court of Burgundy roughly contemporaneous with the poem. This parallel has been rejected, on good grounds, but the geography is real enough, for Vergy lies some fifteen miles south-west of Dijon, and the neighbouring castle of Argilly belonged at that time to the dukes of Burgundy. It may well be that some scandal of the day furnished the poet with this or that detail. One would be tempted to see the little dog as one such, but he may equally well have come from the Tristan legend to which the poet makes the routine reference.

If the plot in its basic outline was not novel, no more so are the characters. On the one hand are the lovers, stock figures both, though the chatelaine is interestingly conceived, on the other the duchess, representing the *losengier*, the tale-bearing, envious felon, who in male or female guise is always present to threaten the fragile happiness of courtly lovers. What then lifts the story out of the common rut and sets it on such a pinnacle of excellence? Firstly the psychological insight, the delicacy with which emotions are explored and set forth, and the admirable portrayal of the duchess whose underhand manoeuvres bring the house of cards tumbling about the lovers' ears. Secondly the figure of the duke, honourable, fair-minded, but culpably weak, caught between the upper and nether millstones of his promise to the knight and his inability to resist his wife's emotional blackmail. And finally the composition and the style. The action, entirely motivated from within, proceeds inexorably towards its climax. It is the lovers themselves who tie the metaphorical noose about their necks: the knight by entrusting the secret of his love to a man who proves himself untrustworthy, the chatelaine by making that secrecy an absolute condition on which her love, her happiness and ultimately her life depend. She dies because she believes herself betrayed, and sees no future for herself but as an object of mockery and scorn, slighted by her lover, triumphed over by the duchess, her honour and good repute lost past recovery. And yet, so selfless is her devotion to the knight that she dies praying for his honour and renown, those very qualities which, forfeited, make living unthinkable. Thus love, however genuine and inward (and who could doubt the depth and sincerity of this passion), is inseparably bound up with outward appearances, with the observance of rules and criteria laid down by a society from which it is inconceivable to opt out. It was not bodily discomfort or waning ardour that determined Béroul's Tristan and Yseult to renounce their life in the forest, but the sense of the sacrifice that each was making for the other in terms of rights and duties and position.

The duke's revenge and expiatory pilgrimage are the acts of a man only too well aware of his own guilt. Indeed each of the four characters is responsible in varying degrees for the ruin that overtakes them all. The only weakness in an otherwise flawlessly structured work is the fortuitous presence of the servant girl hidden in the closet, who, having kept as mum as a mouse while the lady delivers herself of her last monologue and dies, appears at the end like a jack-in-the-box to deliver up the secrets unwittingly confided to her bosom. One sees the reason for the artifice, but it creaks a bit none the less.

The style is uniformly polished with none of the colloquialisms affected by Jean Renart. If in some ways it is less mannered than Renart's it lacks too his earthy realism and vivacity. The conversations between the duke and duchess are admirably rendered with just enough of irony to lighten the underlying melancholy of the theme. The lady's monologue is a great set-piece in the best rhetorical manner, but it must be admitted that it is finely done and in the text attains a genuine lyricism. But the abiding characteristic of the verse is the subtle articulation of the sentences where clause follows clause in a closely knit subordination, which reflects the way in which thoughts, and feelings too, hinge one upon the other – the organic structure of the mental process. I have attempted to render this as faithfully as possible in the translation because it seemed to me a deliberate and wholly successful attempt on the part of the author to recreate in stylistic terms the complex workings of the mind and heart, and indeed the complexity of life itself.

To sum up I should like to quote a passage from Dr Whitehead's illuminating introduction to his edition of the text: '. . . the real significance of the *Chastelaine de Vergi* lies in two things: few other works of the period allow imaginative idealism to be carried to such lengths and in still fewer does a plot at first sight so fantastic and so far removed from normal human experience leave on us an impression of greater plausibility. . . . It would be a gross exaggeration to call the *Chastelaine* the greatest Old French work inspired by the courtly movement, but it is in many ways the most typical and certainly the one which sets the idealism of the movement in its truest light: as an expression, in a special field, of that exalted quality of the mediaeval imagination which forbade it to rest within the bounds of normal experience and sent it off in quest of strange and unattainable goals.'*

* *La Chastelaine de Vergi*, ed. F. Whitehead, p. xxvi.

Select Bibliography

EDITIONS

La Chastelaine de Vergi, ed. Gaston Raynaud, third edition revised by L. Foulet, Classiques Français du Moyen Age, 1921; the text followed in this translation.

La Chastelaine de Vergi, ed. J. Bédier, Paris, 1927, with a modern French translation.

La Chastelaine de Vergi, ed. F. Whitehead, Manchester University Press, 1944, with an excellent introduction and notes.

ARTICLES

G. Raynaud, in *Romania*, 1892.

J. Frappier: 'La Chastelaine de Vergi, Marguerite de Navarre et Bandello', *Pub. de la Fac. des Lettres de l'Université de Strasbourg*, Paris, 1946.

The Chatelaine of Vergy

There exists a class of people who make so good a pretence of loyalty and discretion that one cannot but trust them; yet when it happens that someone opens his heart to them, acquainting them with his love and private affairs, they spread the knowledge abroad and make it a matter for raillery and mirth. And it happens, too, that he who has confided his secret loses his happiness thereby, for the greater the love, the greater the chagrin that true lovers feel when one suspects the other of telling what he should properly conceal. And often there ensues such harm as brings the love affair to a most painful and degrading end, as was the case in Burgundy with a brave and valiant knight and the chatelaine of Vergy, to whom the knight was so passionately attached that she granted him her favours on condition he understood that, at the day and hour of his divulging their love, he would lose both her love and the enjoyment of it. To enable them to enjoy this love they arranged that the knight would resort daily to an orchard at an hour appointed by the lady, and would not stir from a certain nook until he saw a little dog come trotting across the orchard, and then he would go immediately to her chamber, secure in the knowledge that at that time there would be no one there but his mistress. They acted upon this plan for a long time and the secret of their love was so well kept that not a soul knew of it but their two selves.

The knight was handsome and elegant and his valour had won him the friendship of the duke of Burgundy; he came and went freely about the court, and was indeed so assiduous a visitor that the duchess became enamoured of him and gave him such patent signs of her interest that, had his heart not been elsewhere, appearances must have told him of her infatuation. But whatever indications she might give of her feelings, the knight gave none whatsoever of noticing them; in the end she was so galled by this that she accosted him one day and spoke to him in plain terms as follows:

'Sir, you are handsome and valiant – thanks be to God, all say as much – and were well deserving of the favour of some lady whose great position would bring you honour and prestige, for such a mistress would become you well.'

'My lady,' he replied, 'I have given no thought as yet to such ambitions.'

'In faith,' she said, 'delay could spoil your chances, in my opinion. I advise you to try your fortune in the highest quarter, if you see you are well liked there.'

'In faith, my lady,' replied the knight, 'I have no idea why you are saying this nor what it signifies, for I am not a duke or a count that I should set my sights so high, nor am I within an ell of winning the love of any lady so exalted, whatever pains I might take.'

'Perhaps you are,' she answered; 'many a stranger thing happens, and as strange will happen again. Tell me if you know now whether I, who am a lady of high degree, have given you my love.'

The knight replied hurriedly: 'My lady, I do not; but I would welcome your love, so it were consonant with honour. May God preserve me, though, from such love on either of our parts as would bring shame on my lord, for not at any price or in any wise would I commit the outrage of practising so base and treasonous a deception on my true and rightful lord.'

'Fie! Sir Fanciful,' said the lady, much put out, 'and who is asking you to?'

'Ah! my lady, your pardon! I know indeed, I was just making the point.'

The duchess made no further approaches to him, but she was bitterly mortified and out of temper, and resolved if she could to be well and truly revenged. Her indignation was extreme, and that night as she lay in bed beside the duke she started to sigh and then began to weep. The duke immediately asked her what the matter was and insisted that she tell him at once.

'In truth,' she said, 'it makes me miserable to think that great men never know who serves them faithfully and who does not, but confer most benefits and honour on those who play them false without anyone's being aware of it.'

'Upon my faith, madam,' replied the duke, 'I do not know why you say it, but I am certainly guiltless on that score, for I would never knowingly house a traitor.'

'Detest the man then,' said the duchess, naming him, 'who never ceased this livelong day begging me to grant him my favours, and told me that he had been of this mind for a very long time, but had never dared mention it to me. And I bethought myself, dear lord, that I would tell you right away. What is more, it may well be true that he has been thus minded for some time past, for we never heard rumour that he ever loved elsewhere. And I ask you to repay my confidence by defending your honour as and how you know it right.'

The duke, to whom it was most painful news, said to his wife:

'I will deal with this, and quickly too, I fancy.'

The duke spent a comfortless night, unable to sleep a wink on account of the knight for whom he had a great liking. The belief that the other had wronged him, and so forfeited his affection, kept him awake all night. Next morning he rose early and sent for the man whom his wife had made him hate, albeit he had done no wrong. He broached the matter at once and in private:

'Truly,' he said, 'it is a sorry affair, when you have both valour and good looks, that you should be devoid of loyalty. You have deceived me badly on this point, for I have long believed you to be sincerely loyal, at the very least towards me in view of the love I bore you. Where you got so dishonourable a notion as to solicit the duchess's favours I do not know; you are guilty of so vile a betrayal that it would be vain to seek a baser. Quit my land forthwith! For I expel you absolutely and forbid you my entire domain: and if you so much as set foot in it henceforward and should fall into my hands, you can be sure that I would have you hanged.'

When the knight heard this he was so shaken with anger and indignation that he trembled in every limb, bethinking himself of his mistress whose favours he knew he could only enjoy if he could move unchecked about the land from which the duke wished to banish him; furthermore it hurt him acutely that his lord should hold him, and without cause, for a disloyal traitor; all in all he was in such distress that he felt like a man betrayed and as good as slain.

'My lord,' he said, 'for God's sake, grace! do not believe or imagine for a minute that I would ever make so bold: what you mistakenly impute to me never once crossed my mind; and whoever told you so did wrong.'

'It is no use your denying it,' said the duke, 'nor can it be denied. She herself told me how and in what way you solicited and entreated her, like the envious traitor you are; and it may well be you said something more which she is keeping to herself.'

'My lady said what it pleased her to say,' replied the other with a heavy heart.

'There is no use your denying it.'

'There is no use my saying anything at all, yet there is nothing I would not do, so I were believed, for none of this took place.'

'Upon my soul, it did,' said the duke, remembering his wife; for he felt absolutely sure that his wife was telling him the truth, having never heard it rumoured that the knight loved elsewhere. This prompted him to say:

'If you would swear upon your solemn oath that you would give me a truthful answer to what I asked you, your reply would tell me for certain whether or no you had done what I suspect you of.'

The knight, whose sole ambition and desire it was to dispel the unmerited anger which his lord felt towards him, and who apprehended the loss he would sustain in leaving the country where the most charming of women dwelled, replied that he would do without fail everything the duke suggested, for he had no thought or suspicion of what the other had in mind, and his torment prevented his guessing what the duke wished to ask beyond this initial request. This he swore to in the manner agreed, and the duke accepted his oath and proceeded at once to say to him:

'Know then in very truth that the fact that I have loved you in the past with a discerning heart altogether prevents my believing you guilty of such perfidy and misconduct as the duchess tells me of. Nor would I grant there being a grain of truth in it were I not led to believe it and filled with dire misgivings by my observing in your behaviour and appearance a certain elegance and other signs which point unmistakably to your being in love with someone; and when furthermore no maiden or lady is seen to be the subject of your love, I think to myself that my wife must be the one, who tells me that you solicit her favours. And nothing that anyone can do will ever sway me from my conviction that this is how things stand, unless you prove to me that you are in love with another, by letting me know, without any room for doubt, the whole truth of the affair. And if you are not willing to do this, then quit my country on the spot, as a man forsworn!'

The knight was at a nonplus, in that the alternatives offered him were so harsh that he considered each to be a death-sentence; for if he revealed the whole truth, as he must if he were not to perjure himself, and committed the crime of breaking the compact he had with his lady and mistress, he would be a dead man, for he was assured of losing her if she discovered his betrayal; yet not telling the duke the truth would make him a perjurer and forswearer, and lose him the country and his mistress too; the former loss were trifling enough, could he but keep his mistress whom he feared more than anything else to lose. The constant recollection of the joy and bliss he had known in her arms led him to wonder, if he lost her either by wronging her or through being unable to take her with him, how he would ever survive without her. Thus he found himself in the very plight described in the verse of a song by the castellan of Couci, whose heart was utterly possessed by love:

> O Love, most hard I find it to forgo
> The sweet felicity and company
> And the soft glances oft on me bestowed
> By her who was my mistress and my love.
> When I bethink me of her simple grace
> And the sweet words she used to say to me,
> How can my heart live on within my breast?
> In tarrying there it shows itself too base.[1]

The knight, in this agony of mind, did not know whether to tell the duke the truth, or to lie and leave the country; and while he was in this mental travail, unable to decide which course would stand him in best stead, he worked himself to such a pitch of misery that tears welled into his eyes, and spilling over, bathed his cheeks. This sight did nothing to cheer the duke, who thought there was something which the knight dared not confess to him, and he said to him hurriedly:

'I see plainly that you do not trust me as much as you ought. Do you believe that if you told me of your affair in confidence I would repeat it to anybody? There is no question but I would first see all my teeth drawn one by one.'

'Ah, my lord, have pity! I do not know what I ought to say nor what will become of me; but I would sooner die than lose what I must lose had I told you the truth; for if it came to her knowledge that I had confessed it at any living moment . . .!'

The duke broke in:

'I swear to you upon my life and soul and by the love and faith I owe you on your homage, that as long as I live no hint of your affair will be given by word or look or manner to any living creature.'

At that the knight said, weeping:

'My lord, I will tell it you on that condition: I love your niece of Vergy and she loves me, as deeply as can be.'

'Tell me then,' said the duke, 'seeing you want the affair kept dark, did no one know of this but you two?'

'No,' said the knight, 'not a soul in the world.'

'This is unheard of,' said the duke; 'how do you manage it then, and how do you fix a time and place?'

'Faith, my lord,' said the other, 'by a stratagem with which I will acquaint you fully, now that you know so much about our affair.'

Thereupon he related to him all his comings and goings, the initial agreement, and the arrangement with the little dog, after which the duke said:

'Be good enough at your next tryst to let me keep you company on your way, for I wish to know without equivocation if the affair is really as you say; my niece, for her part, will know nothing about it.'

'My lord,' replied the knight, 'you have my ready consent, as long as it does not irk or inconvenience you, and, please you to know, I shall be going this night.'

The duke replied that he would go too, and that, far from irking him, it would be a pleasure and a diversion. Between them they settled the place where they would meet on foot.

It was not far from their meeting place to where the duke's niece lived, so they set out as soon as night had fallen and made their way to the garden, where the duke had not long to wait before he saw his niece's little dog come trotting across to the end of the orchard where he found the knight who made a great fuss of him. The knight left the duke and was on his way at once, while the latter walked in his wake to within a short distance of the chamber, and stopped short; there he concealed himself as best he could and proved his skill in the art, taking cover behind a huge, spreading tree which served him in the manner of a shield. It was from this vantage point that he saw the knight enter the chamber. First he saw his niece emerge from it, coming out into a little meadow to meet her lover; he heard, too, her cry of delight and saw how she greeted him with outstretched arms as soon as she caught sight of him.[2] Running out of the chamber towards him she threw her fair arms round him and kissed him more than a hundred times before she spoke at any length. He returned her kisses and embraces, saying:

'My lady, my sweet, my love, my mistress dear, my hope and all that I adore, believe me I have hungered to hold you as I hold you now each day since I last did so.'

She said in turn:

'Sweet lord, sweet friend, my sweetest love, not a day nor an hour has passed since then when I have not chafed at the waiting, but I know neither grief nor care now that I have my heart's desire, and you are here with me, hale and happy, so most welcome!'

'And you well met!' replied her lover.

Each word they spoke before going in was overheard by the duke, leaning against the tree close by. He recognized his niece by voice and feature quite clearly enough to be freed of all his doubts and to hold the duchess a liar in respect of what she had told him; and this pleased him greatly. It was plain to him now that the knight was quite guiltless of the wrong he had suspected him of. He stayed positioned there all that night, while the lady and the knight lay in one bed within, together but not asleep, enjoying such pleasure and delight as it neither befits me to describe, nor any man to hear about unless he hopes to have such joy as Love gives to true lovers when he requites love's pains. For if a man hears about such joy while he has no expectation of attaining it, he cannot begin to understand it, since his heart is not in Love's subjection; for none would ever know what the having of such joy is worth unless Love himself gave the knowledge. Nor does this blessing fall to every man's lot; for it is joy unmarred, and ease and gladness: but the truth of it is that it lasts but a moment, or so thinks every lover who enjoys it; for such is his delight in loving that however long it lasted, if a night became a week, the week a month, the month a year, and one year three, and three years twenty, and twenty years a hundred, when it came to the end he would still want dusk to fall on that last night, sooner than see dawn break. Such was the train of thought of the man for whom the duke stood waiting; for before day broke he had to leave, and his mistress came with him to the door. There the duke saw kisses given and returned at parting, and much sighing and weeping as the lovers took their leave. Many a tear was shed there, and he heard, too, a time arranged for a future meeting. So it was that the knight left, and the lady shut the door, but as long as she could see him her lovely eyes accompanied him on his way, in default of anything better.

The duke set off as soon as he saw the door close, and soon overtook the knight, who was busy complaining to himself that the night had been too short for his liking. Meanwhile the lady he had left was musing and murmuring in a similar vein, feeling that the night had cheated her of her pleasure and rueing the coming of dawn. The knight was thinking such thoughts and voicing such complaints when the duke, catching up with him, embraced him with manifest delight and said to him:

'I vow to you that I will always love you from now on, and will never bear you malice again; for you have told me the truth in every respect without one word of falsehood.'

'My lord,' said the other, 'I am beholden to you! But for the love of God I ask and beg of you that it please you to keep this matter to yourself, for I should lose love and joy and ease, and would die a certain death, if I knew that it were to come to the ears of any save yourself!'

'Say no more,' replied the duke; 'rest assured that your secret will be so well kept that not a soul will learn of it through me.'

Thus conversing, they arrived back at their point of departure. And that same day, when they came to dine, the duke showed himself more gracious to the knight than ever before, which of a truth made the duchess so sick with rage that she rose from the table and, feigning a sudden indisposition, went to lie on her bed, where she found little enough enjoyment. The duke, after eating and washing his hands and making agreeably merry, went directly to see his wife. Getting her to sit up on the bed, he ordered everyone else to leave the room, which at his behest they immediately did; thereupon he asked her outright the cause of her indisposition and what it was that had ailed her.

'As God is my help,' she answered, 'I had no fears, when I sat down just now to dine, that I would find so little sense and judgement in you as you showed in increasing your cordiality to the man who, as I told you, is bent on shaming and disgracing me: and when I saw you being even more gracious to him than before, I was so upset and angry that I could not stay there another moment.'

'Ah! my sweet love,' said the duke, 'be it known to you that nothing you or anyone else might say would make me believe that what you told me ever, by any chance, took place. On the contrary, I have learned enough of his affairs to know him to be quite innocent even to the thought of it; and you are never to ask me any more about it.'

With that the duke went out, leaving his wife with plenty to think on: for she would never know an hour's peace of mind as long as she lived, until she learned more of the matter about which the duke had forbidden her to ask; and vainly forbidden at that, for she was covertly devising a scheme which would enable her to find out for sure, if she resigned herself until she had the duke in her arms that night: for she knew for a certainty that she would get her own way with him more easily in the course of such dalliance

than at any other time. So she bided her time accordingly, and when
the duke came to bed, she shifted over to the far side, acting as if she
were in no mood for his attentions, for she was well aware that the
means to get the whip-hand over her husband was by making a
show of pique. She behaved, therefore, in the way best calculated
to persuade the duke that she was in high dudgeon; and so, without
his having done more than kiss her, she said to him:

'It is very deceitful and false and disloyal of you to make a
show of loving me, you who have never, ever truly loved me: for
a long time I was foolish enough to take you at your word, since
you told me many a time that you loved me with a true heart; but I
realized today that I have been abused in this.'

'Did you?' said the duke. 'How so?'

'Upon my faith,' replied the lady, bent on mischief, 'just now
you told me not to presume to question you on that matter you
now know all about.'

'What matter, my sweet, for heaven's sake?'

'What that fellow related to you, those lies and fables that he
made you believe. But I am not interested in knowing what it was,
for I have decided that there is little use my loving you with a true
and constant heart: for I never had any privy knowledge, good or
ill, that I did not share with you on the spot; and now I see that
you, thank you kindly, are keeping your thoughts from me. And
be it most clearly known to you that I will never put the same trust
in you again, nor feel towards you as I have in the past.'

With that the duchess began to weep and sigh, straining herself
to the utmost. And the duke felt so sorry for her that he said:

'My sweetheart, I would give anything not to suffer your anger
or your resentment: but understand that I cannot divulge what you
want me to tell you without being guilty of the grossest treachery.'

She retorted at once:

'And do not tell it me either, my lord, for it is obvious to me
from your attitude that you do not trust me to keep your secret;
and you may as well know that I am most amazed: for you never
heard of my venting any secret, great or small, which you had
confided to me. And I assure you in all good faith that such a thing
will never happen as long as I live.'

Having said that, she wept some more, and the duke kissed and embraced her, so discomposed and wretched that he could not keep any longer from revealing what was on his mind. So he said to her then:

'Dear lady, upon my soul, I do not know what to do, for I have such confidence and faith in you, that I ought not to keep anything from you that comes to my ears or knowledge; but I beg you not to breathe a word of it: I tell you this much for your understanding, that if you ever betray me it will cost you your life.'

'I accept that readily,' she answered; 'it is out of the question that I should do anything that might offend you.'

Because he loved her, he believed her, accepting what she said as the truth, and told her then the whole story of his niece, how he had learned it from the knight, and how the two of them had stood alone in the corner of the orchard, when the little dog came across to them; he described the lovers' entrances and exits, and finally kept back nothing of what he had seen and heard. When the duchess heard that he who had spurned her affections loved a woman of lesser degree, she could have died of mortification; she gave no outward sign of it, however, but promised the duke her silence and agreed that, should the affair be divulged by her, he might hang her with a rope round her neck. Meanwhile she was already itching to speak to the woman whom she hated from the moment she knew her to be loved of him who shamed and affronted her merely, as she thought, by refusing to become her lover. She made up her mind that if she found a time and a place for speaking to the duke's niece, she would broach the matter at once, sparing no venomous detail.

But she never did find her occasion until the following Whitsun-tide came round, when the duke held his first high court, and sent out summonses to all the ladies of the land, and first and foremost to his niece, the chatelaine of Vergy. When the duchess set eyes on the woman she hated above all others her blood boiled within her. She managed, however, to hide her feelings and received her more graciously than she ever had before: she was burning, though, to tell her what was making her fume in secret, and it cost her dear to wait. So, on Whit Sunday, when the tables had been removed, the duchess led the ladies to her chamber, so that they might adorn themselves in privacy before coming in all their elegance to the dances. There, seeing her opportunity, she found herself quite unable to bottle up her words, and remarked as though in banter:

'Chatelaine, look to your beauty, for you have a good friend who is both handsome and valiant.'

The other replied very simply: 'In truth, I do not know what friend you can mean, my lady, for I have no wish to have any friend, save such as were wholly compatible both with my honour and with that of my lord.'

'I am sure that is so,' said the duchess; 'howbeit, you are a clever mistress to have learned the art of training the little dog.'

The other ladies overheard the exchange, but without understanding its purport, and in company with the duchess they went back and took part in the dancing.

The chatelaine stayed behind, pale with anger, and sick and shaken to her heart's core. She entered a closet where a young girl, unobserved by her, was lying at the foot of the bed. In great distress she let herself fall on the bed and there cried out, distraught:

'Ah! God in heaven, have pity! What can it be that I heard? My lady shamed me with having trained my little dog? That is something she cannot have learned from anyone, as I know full well, save from the one I loved and who has betrayed my trust; nor would he ever have told her that unless he were on intimate terms with her, and loved her beyond question more than me, whom he has thus betrayed. His breaking faith with me makes it plain he does not love me. Dear God! and I loved him as much as any creature could love another, so much that I could think of nothing else by day or night, not for a single hour. For he was joy and gladness to me, delight and pleasure and solace and heart's ease. How could I keep from thinking of him in his absence! Ah! dear friend, how did this come about? What can have happened to you, to make you false to me? As God is my help, I thought you would be truer to me than Tristan was to Iseult; and I loved you more by half, may God have pity on me, than I loved myself. Never from first to last was I guilty in thought, word or deed of any offence, great or small, which could warrant your hating me or betraying me so ignobly as to break up our love to love another, and to forsake me and disclose the affair between us two. Alas, dear friend, I am lost in wonderment, for, so help me God! my heart was never thus disposed towards you; for had God offered me all the world, and His heaven and paradise besides, I'd not have accepted, had it meant losing you thereby; for you were my riches, health and happiness, and as long as my poor heart knew that there was some love for me in yours, there was nothing that had the power to hurt me. Alas for true love! who would have thought that the man who said, when we were together, and I at pains to gratify his every wish, that he was wholly mine and held me as his lady, to serve body and soul, would ever be guilty of such dereliction? And he said it so sweetly that I really believed him and never would have thought that, were it for duchess or for queen, he could have found it in his heart to bear me malice or hatred; for loving him was such delight that I took his feelings for my own. I thought, too, that he saw his love for me lasting as long as he lived. For my nature is such that, had he died before me, I know, so deeply did I love him, that I would not have survived him long, for I'd liefer be dead along with him than live without ever seeing him again. Alas for true love! is it right then that he should thus have disclosed our secret? And lose me in the doing, since at my first bestowing my love I told him, and made it a clear condition, that he would lose me the moment he breathed a word of our affair. And now that it's I who have lost him first, I cannot, after such a blow, live on without the one whose loss I mourn, nor do I seek or wish it. I take no pleasure in my life; on the contrary I pray that God may suffer me to die and that, as truly as I truly loved him who has driven me to this, He may have pity on my soul, and grant that he who wrongfully betrayed me and delivered me up to death, and whom I now forgive, have honour and renown. And it seems to me that, coming as it does through him, my death cannot be other than sweet, and when I recall his love, dying for him presents no hardship for me.'

With that the chatelaine fell silent, save that she added in a sigh: 'Sweet friend, I commend you to God's keeping.'

So saying, she pressed both hands to her breast, her heart failed her, and the colour drained from her face as she swooned in anguish and lay back lifeless on the bed, pale, and wan, and dead. All this, however, remained unknown to her lover, who was disporting himself in the hall in the diverse dances;[3] howbeit, the scene afforded him no pleasure, since she on whom his heart was bestowed was nowhere to be seen, and in his astonishment he whispered to the duke:

'My lord, how is it that your niece has tarried so long that she is not yet come to the dances? Have you shut her away, I wonder?'

The duke, who had not noticed her absence, glanced round the circle of dancers; then, drawing the knight towards him by the hand, he made off straight for the chamber; when he failed to find her there he bade and urged the knight to look for her in the closet, wishing in this way to allow the two of them the pleasure of kissing and embracing within. The knight, greatly obliged to him, entered the closet where his mistress was lying prone and deathly pale upon the bed. With privacy and leisure thus ensured, he took her at once in his arms and kissed her, but found her lips cold and her flesh pallid and unyielding, and realized from the appearance of her body that she was stone dead.

Immediately he cried out aghast:

'What is this? Alas, is my love dead?'

At that the girl who had been lying at the foot of the bed jumped up, saying:

'Indeed, sir, I think she must be dead, for she asked for nothing else since coming here, she was so wrought up over my lady's badgering her about her lover, and she taunted her, too, about a little dog, which caused her such distress as grew past bearing.'

The knight, when he heard these words and realized that what he had told the duke had killed his mistress, was seized with wild despair:

'Alas!' he cried, 'my own sweet love, the most gracious and noblest and best that ever was, and the most loyal too, I have killed you like the faithless traitor that I am! It is I who by rights should have suffered for this business, so that you were spared all hurt; but you were so true of heart that you took it upon yourself, forestalling me. But I shall do justice on myself for the treachery I committed.'

Therewith, unsheathing a sword that was hanging from a pillar, he plunged it into his breast and, shedding his heart's blood, fell dead on his mistress' body.

At the sight of the lifeless corpses the girl rushed out in panic. Encountering the duke she told him, without concealing a detail, everything she had seen and heard: how the affair had originated, and even to the training of the little dog which the duchess had spoken of. Imagine the duke's fury: he entered the closet on the spot and drew from the knight's body the sword with which he had killed himself. Thereupon, wasting no words on the way, he dashed straight off to the dancing and the duchess, and there and then made good his promise to her, bringing the naked sword he was holding down on her head with never a word spoken, so enraged was he. The duchess fell at his feet in the sight of all his vassals from round about, which cast a sorry blight on the revelling of the assembled knights who had been enjoying themselves in festive spirit. Then the duke, forthwith, in the hearing of all who cared to listen, related the whole affair in open court. There was no one there who did not weep to hear it, and especially when they saw the two lovers lying dead, and the duchess too. The court dispersed in grief and gloom and hideous wretchedness, and the following day the duke had the lovers buried in one tomb, and the duchess laid elsewhere. But the incident left him so bitter at heart that he was never heard to laugh again; shortly after he took the cross and left for the Holy Land where he became a Templar, and never more returned.

Ah, God! this whole calamity and doom sprang from the knight's being so misguided as to tell what it behoved him to keep quiet, and what his mistress had forbidden him to reveal as long as he wanted to retain her love. This example should teach us to conceal our love with such cunning as comes of bearing ever in mind that disclosure gains us nothing, while secrecy has everything to commend it. He who observes this rule is proof against the attacks of those false, prying knaves who pry into the loves of other folk.

NOTES

p. 24, note 1.   *Qui vauroit bons vers oïr*
                       Del deport du viel antif
                       De deus biax enfans petis,
                       Nicholete et Aucassins.

The second line of *Aucassin and Nicolette* has remained something of an enigma ever since scholarly attention was first focused on the work. The usual meaning of '*deport*' is pleasure, but who or what is meant by the '*viel antif*', literally the old ancient? It has been variously suggested that the author, in his declining years, was thus referring to himself; that it was his proper name, or rather sobriquet; that it refers to his real or imaginary source. Again, was the pleasure his, or that which he hoped to give his readers? Whichever way the line is construed the sense remains obscure. I have therefore adopted Professor Pelan's suggestion that '*deport*' should in fact be read '*depart*'. This is not a purely arbitrary hypothesis; the final downstroke of the '*a*' is missing in other words where the context makes it quite clear that an '*a*' and not an '*o*' was intended. The reading '*depart*', meaning separation, gives us the following lines: 'about the separation by the very old man of two fair youngsters'. Since the story is indeed about the efforts of the hero's father, Count Garin, to prevent the marriage of Aucassin and Nicolette, and since the author tells us in the very next section that the said count was old and feeble, this solution has at the very least the merit of restoring sense to a passage which had little enough before. Cf. M. Pelan, 'Le Deport du Viel Antif', in *Neuphilologische Mitteilungen*, 1960.

p. 25, note 2.   *De Nicole le bien faite*
                       Nus hom ne l'en puet retraire
                       Que ses peres ne li laisse
                       Et sa mere le manace:

Depending on the grammatical function one attributes to '*que*' in the third line and how, in consequence, one punctuates the passage, various meanings are possible. It could for example be read: None can wean him from lissom Nicolette *whom* his father will not give to him. If '*que*' is a conjunction it could mean *for*, *although*, or *save that* (cf. Roques, notes to 1954 edition).

p. 26, note 3. Actually Cartagena, a town on the east coast of Spain, then under Moorish rule. The text has 'Cartage' throughout, and I have kept it too, on account of its associations with exotic wealth and splendour, of which the author was doubtless well aware – *viz.* the popular saying: '*aussi riche que le roi de Carthage*'.

p. 28, note 4. '*Faide vous en sera demandee*'. *La faide* enshrined the legal right to private vengeance, in the circumstances a somewhat comic notion.

p. 28, note 5. The text has '*li vairs et li gris*'. These were costly furs much used by the nobles for trimming robes. In association, as here, the words are symbolic of luxury and riches, and I have tried to find a couplet with similar overtones.

p. 34, note 6. '*Soupe en maserin*'. Not, as has been suggested, some sort of soup, which would indeed make a bizarre analogy, but a sop probably dipped in spiced and sweetened wine, delectable no doubt to the accustomed palate. A mazer was a drinking cup, usually of maple wood.

p. 40, note 7. '*S'endormi jusqu'au demain a haute prime*'. The canonical hour of prime falls at 6 a.m. The adjective '*haut*' refers to the place of the sun in the sky, rising during the morning, and indicates therefore a time between prime and terce (9 a.m.). Cf. Suchier's 1913 edition, pp. 54–5.

p. 41, note 8. Most editors take '*le garris*' to be the *garrigue*, the hills of Provence with their typical sparse vegetation, though Suchier held it to represent the ilex, or evergreen oak, characteristic of that region.

p. 46, note 9. The words in brackets are missing in the text due to a tear in the manuscript. Bourdillon reconstituted the sentence with the help of a few remaining letters.

p. 47, note 10. The same lacuna accounts for the missing verses here. Parts of the words '*lumiere*' and '*soir*' in line 6 encouraged H. Suchier to indulge in some inspired guess-work which, for present purposes, seemed preferable to the rows of little dots left by other editors.

p. 49, note 11. Although there is no obvious lacuna in the manuscript it is clear from the sense that there has been an omission on the part of the scribe, distracted by the same word, '*rive*', appearing at the end of two consecutive sentences. I have followed Bourdillon's version.

p. 49, note 12. The text has Torelore. Sainte-Palaye, writing in the eighteenth century, affirmed that men who knew the region well identified Torelore with Aigues-Mortes, a sea-port in the time of Saint Louis, and still commonly known in his own day as the '*pays de Turelure*' on account of the singularities of the place and its inhabitants (cf. Suchier, p. 68). Whether or not the author of *Aucassin and Nicolette* had any specific town or region in mind, it is plain that he thought of his Torelore first and foremost as a fantastical country where all accepted customs and conventions are turned upside down. There Aucassin, held for a fool in his own land, appears as a sage in a land of fools.

p. 50, note 13. A reference to the custom known as the couvade, whereby when a woman bears a child the husband takes to his bed and is tended as though it were he who had given birth. It is probable that the author derived his knowledge, directly or indirectly, from the account given by Strabo in the ninth century.

p. 52, note 14. The actual line is: '*Ne deduis de la nimpole*', i.e. the pleasures of a certain board game, perhaps akin to draughts.

p. 56, note 15. Old French *esclaire*. One suspects that the appositeness of the name (the verb *esclairier* means to lighten) dictated the author's choice of simple.

THE LAY OF THE REFLECTION

p. 64, note 1. A reference to the *Roman de l'Escoufle*.

p. 64, note 2. The '*Eslit*', or '*élu*', here referred to was probably Miles of Nanteuil, elected to the bishopric of Beauvais in 1217. Jean Renart had already dedicated *Guillaume de Dôle* to him at some unknown but earlier date. Mme Lejeune, basing her conjecture on another passage in the *Lay*, where Renart refers to the possibility of being 'captured by the Turks and taken off to Cairo', assumes that the poet accompanied his patron on the Fifth Crusade, when Miles was in fact captured by the Sultan at the siege of Damietta in 1219 and held prisoner in Cairo until 1221. The work would therefore have been written in his immediate entourage, possibly during a sojourn at Acre, and certainly before his consecration in Rome which took place on his homeward journey during the winter 1221–2. Attractive though the theory is, the evidence is somewhat flimsy, and it would be safer to fix the date of composition within the wider limits set by the period 1219 to 1222, without giving undue weight to the poet's hypothetical visit to the Holy Land.

p. 64, note 3. The whole passage as printed by Orr reads as follows:

> v. 46　　*On dit: qui bien nage bien rime;*
> *Qui de haute mer vient a rive,*
> *Fox est së a la mer estrive.*
> *Qui a port de bien dïre arrive,*
> *Miex l'em prisent roi et conte.*

The first line contains an untranslatable pun on the verb *rimer*, which means both to rhyme and to steer. The manuscript E, which forms the basis of Orr's edition, gives only the lines 1, 2, 3 and 5. The other manuscripts omit line 3 and replace it by line 4. The rhyme pattern suggests that the original text featured either two lines, or possibly four, ending in *-ive*; three would be most exceptional. Orr offers the following rendering of the whole: ' "Steer well, rhyme well", they say. "He who comes to shore from the high seas is a fool if he chides the waves. He who makes the haven of good poesy wins higher praise from counts and kings (i.e. the discerning)" ' (cf. Orr, op. cit., Notes, p. 32). This makes adequate sense but does not seem entirely logical in its development. My version has nothing but clarity to recommend it, but is the best I can do with a clearly corrupt text.

p. 65, note 4. Literally from Châlons to Le Perche, the approximate limits of the then royal domain.

p. 65, note 5. cf. Orr, p. 34: 'Possibly a popular expression quite in Jean Renart's manner: to like Monday, when the week's work begins, would already be a sign of energy, to wish that there were two Mondays in every week a good deal more so. . . . One must however take into account the fact that . . . tournaments commonly began on Mondays.'

p. 66, note 6. A reference to an episode in the Tristan legend featured in the text known as the 'Berne Folie'. This and the two other allusions in the *Lay* indicate Jean Renart's admiration for the tale of Tristan and Yseult, borne out by references to it in his other works. Since, however, the two known French versions of the story only survive in fragmentary form (not to mention that of Chrétien de Troyes, entirely lost) it is impossible to know which, if either, he was referring to.

p. 68, note 7. The various manuscripts give differing versions of this line. E's reading: '*A tel voiage, tel tencon!*' seems to mean: 'For such an errand, such a rivalry'. I have preferred F's version: '*A tel voiage tel chanson*', which is closer to Bédier's translation: '*Chanson bien digne d'un tel voyage!*'

p. 71, note 8. '*Certes, dame, se vos fussiez . . .*' Orr considers E's version rather weak and prefers that of F which he gives among other variants: '*Dieu, naje! se vos fussiez . . .*'

p. 72, note 9.   *Je sui toz en vostre dangier*
                    Qanque jë ai force et pooir,

literally, 'I am entirely at your disposal in so far as I have strength and power' (Orr, p. 48). On the other hand A has '*Qanques je ai, force et pooir*', which would mean, taking Bédier's punctuation: 'Whatever I have of strength and power is wholly at your disposal.'

p. 73, note 10.   *Toz li sans dusqu'au doit mainuel*
                    De son pié li esvanoï.

A burlesque of the conventional figure of blood draining from the face as a result of shock or emotion, typical of the poet's manner.

p. 75, note 11. The sense of these five lines of the text as printed by Orr is somewhat strained. He himself states: 'F's version of the whole passage . . . seems much happier.' I have therefore followed this version as given in the variants, p. 54.

p. 77, note 12.   '*Il m'est vis que vos m'apreingniez,*'
                    Fet il, 'a chanter de Renart.'

All the other manuscripts, saving F which has something totally different, read '*a chanter de Bernart*'. Bernart was the name of the ass in the *Chanson de Renart*, and there is an expression '*chanter d'autre Bernart*', meaning to change one's tune. Presumably, therefore, '*chanter de Bernart*' is to bray, hence to repeat oneself. Orr, who offers this interpretation, also thinks it possible that E's reading was a deliberate pun by the poet on his own name (Orr, p. 57).

p. 77, note 13. Another case of conflicting manuscript reading. I have adopted the version which Professor Orr considers likely to have been the correct one: '*Ainz me lairoie a une hart Poncier le col que jel preïsse.*'

p. 79, note 14. Jean Renart, typically, ends his poem on what seems to be a pun: '*Contez, vos qui savez de nombre,*' or in other words: '*Vous qui savez compter, racontez!*'

THE CHATELAINE OF VERGY

p. 142, note 1. This stanza is indeed taken from the song beginning '*A vos, amant, plus k'a nule autre gent*' composed by Gui de Coucy, a *trouvère* of distinction. Castellan of Coucy in the last years of the twelfth century, he embarked on the Fourth Crusade and, according to the chronicler Villehardouin, died at sea in 1203. It was Jean Renart who first had the idea of incorporating into the narrative of his *Guillaume de Dôle* verses taken from the most popular lyrics of his day. At least two other works besides *The Chatelaine of Vergy* witness to its having become a literary fashion.

p. 144, note 2. In the text the poet seems to have the knight entering the castle and the lady subsequently coming out to meet him, hardly a logical sequence of events. In point of fact he is giving a general picture and then proceeding to detail it, a common practice of his time. By introducing the word 'first' I have tried to circumvent the difficulty.

p. 151, note 3.   *qui se deduisoit en la sale*
                            a la carole et dansse et bale.

These terms have no equivalents in modern English, being the names of different types of dance. The *carole* was a round dance, often accompanied by singing (*viz.* the English 'carol' where only the singing element has survived), the *danse* was more stately and processional, while the last, from its association with the verb *baler*, to leap, would presumably have been the most vivacious of the three. I am indebted to Mrs Ann Harding for the above distinctions. The two other references to dances in the text both have the term *carole* – perhaps the most popular variety.